# Isese

*The Ultimate Guide to Ancestral Spiritual Tradition, Ifa Divination, Yoruba, Odu, Iwa, Asafo, and Orishas*

© Copyright 2023 — All rights reserved.

The content contained within this book may not be reproduced, duplicated, or transmitted without direct written permission from the author or the publisher.

Under no circumstances will any blame or legal responsibility be held against the publisher, or author, for any damages, reparation, or monetary loss due to the information contained within this book, either directly or indirectly.

**Legal Notice:**

This book is copyright protected. It is only for personal use. You cannot amend, distribute, sell, use, quote, or paraphrase any part of the content within this book without the consent of the author or publisher.

**Disclaimer Notice:**

Please note the information contained within this document is for educational and entertainment purposes only. All effort has been executed to present accurate, up-to-date, reliable, and complete information. No warranties of any kind are declared or implied. Readers acknowledge that the author is not engaging in the rendering of legal, financial, medical, or professional advice. The content within this book has been derived from various sources. Please consult a licensed professional before attempting any techniques outlined in this book.

By reading this document, the reader agrees that under no circumstances is the author responsible for any losses, direct or indirect, that are incurred as a result of the use of the information contained within this document, including, but not limited to, errors, omissions, or inaccuracies.

# Your Free Gift
# (only available for a limited time)

Thanks for getting this book! If you want to learn more about various spirituality topics, then join Mari Silva's community and get a free guided meditation MP3 for awakening your third eye. This guided meditation mp3 is designed to open and strengthen ones third eye so you can experience a higher state of consciousness. Simply visit the link below the image to get started.

https://spiritualityspot.com/meditation

# Table of Contents

INTRODUCTION ........1
CHAPTER 1: WHAT IS ISESE? ........3
CHAPTER 2: OLODUMARE, THE COSMOS, AND YOU ........13
CHAPTER 3: ODU IFA, THE DIVINE SCRIPTURE ........23
CHAPTER 4: PRACTICING IFA DIVINATION ........33
CHAPTER 5: THE SEVEN GREAT ORISHAS ........44
CHAPTER 6: WALK THE PATH OF YOUR ANCESTORS ........62
CHAPTER 7: HONORING YOUR ANCESTORS ........69
CHAPTER 8: WHAT ASAFO FLAGS CAN TEACH ........77
CHAPTER 9: IWA, OR BUILDING A STRONG CHARACTER ........84
CHAPTER 10: PRACTICING ISESE EVERY DAY ........91
BONUS: AN ISESE GLOSSARY ........98
CONCLUSION ........101
HERE'S ANOTHER BOOK BY MARI SILVA THAT YOU MIGHT LIKE ........103
YOUR FREE GIFT (ONLY AVAILABLE FOR A LIMITED TIME) ........104
BIBLIOGRAPHY ........105

# Introduction

Do you want to learn more about Isese and its origins? Have you ever wondered how to follow its path? If so, this book is for you.

Isese is a set of practices that were traditionally used by the Yoruba people of Nigeria to maintain mental and physical health, as well as to cleanse the body and prepare it for special occasions. The word Isese means "purification," and these practices aim to purify the body and soul. Isese includes internal and external cleansing, dietary restrictions, meditation, and prayer. Many Yoruba people still use these practices today and believe they help bring physical, mental, and spiritual balance. In addition, Isese is often used as a form of preventative medicine, as it is believed to help ward off disease.

In this book, we will explore the history of the Isese and its significance in Yoruba culture. We will discuss the importance of honoring your ancestors and the role of orishas and Odu Ifa in Isese. We will also look at how to practice Isese divination and bring the practice into your everyday life. Finally, we will discuss the role of Iwa in Isese, which is a set of values people must adhere to maintain spiritual balance.

Isese is a traditional Nigerian religion that offers daily opportunities for Africans to connect with the spirit world. The practice of Isese involves communication with ancestors and other spirits through prayer, offerings, and divination. Followers of Isese believe that spirits can help them to navigate the challenges of everyday life.

Isese is usually practiced at home, often early in the morning or late at night. A typical session might involve lighting a candle and praying to one's ancestors. Many believers also keep a shrine for their ancestors in their homes, which might be decorated with photos, statues, or other symbols of respect. The practice of Isese can bring a sense of peace and connection to those who participate. It can also be a way to tap into wisdom from our ancestors that can help us make choices in our own lives. For many Africans, Isese is essential to their cultural heritage and identity.

Regardless of your background, this book will give you the tools and knowledge to live an authentic Isese lifestyle. By the end of this book, you will have a better understanding of Isese and its importance to the Yoruba people. You will also have gained insight into how to follow Isese in your own life, as well as how to use it to promote physical and spiritual balance. The path of Isese can be difficult and challenging at times, but the rewards are worth it in the end. So, if you are ready to begin your journey, come and join us as we explore the wonders of Isese.

# Chapter 1: What Is Isese?

Isese is an ancient African spirituality and religion that has its roots in the Yoruba people of Nigeria and Benin. Over the centuries, it has evolved into a distinct belief system with unique practices. Isese is based on the worship of the Orisa, a pantheon of deities responsible for different aspects of human life. One of the most important aspects of Isese is the use of ritual and ceremony to honor the deities and ask for their guidance and protection. In recent years, there has been a resurgence of interest in Isese among the Yoruba people, and it is now practiced worldwide.

Isese has its roots in the Yoruba people.
*Fastaschool, CC BY-SA 4.0 <https://creativecommons.org/licenses/by-sa/4.0/deed.en> via Wikimedia Commons*
https://commons.wikimedia.org/wiki/File:The_Yoruba_Cultural_Group_Children_of_Fasta_International_School_-_Photo_Session.jpg

This chapter will introduce readers to the core concepts of Isese, provide an overview of its history and cultural context, and explore the structure and practice of Isese and the key figures and symbols associated with the religion. In addition, it will explain the differences between Isese and traditional African spirituality and outline the essential principles of Isese. Finally, readers will be provided with useful tips for pronouncing Yoruba and Isese terms.

## The Origin of Isese

Isese (pronounced as "ee-SEH-shay") is believed to be thousands of years old and belonged to the ancient Yoruba culture, which flourished on the west coast of Africa in present-day Nigeria and Benin. This belief system developed from the indigenous people's traditional religions, a polytheistic faith that honored multiple deities and spirits.

Isese is based on the belief that the spirits of one's ancestors can help or hinder them in their life journey. If they are properly honored and respected, they will intercede on behalf of their living relatives. However, they may bring misfortune or even death if they are not honored. As a result, Isese practitioners put great emphasis on ancestor veneration. They build shrines for their ancestors and make offerings of food, drink, and other items. They also hold festivals and ceremonies in honor of their departed loved ones. By honoring their ancestors, they ensure that they will continue to receive their blessings.

## Where Does Isese Come From?

The word "Isese" can also be translated to "divinity" or "deity," and practitioners believe in a pantheon of gods and goddesses who oversee different aspects of life. Isese is based on the worship of ancestors, and many ceremonies and rituals focus on honoring those who have passed away. Prayer, sacrifice, and divination are also key components of the religion. Isese has been passed down through generations for centuries, and it continues to play an essential role in the lives of its adherents. While the religion may be unfamiliar to some, its rich traditions and history offer a glimpse into the vibrant culture of the Yoruba people.

## The History of Isese

Isese has its roots in the traditional beliefs of the Yoruba people of Nigeria and Dahomey (now Benin). Isese is based on the belief that there is a supreme creator god, Olorun, who is responsible for everything that exists. Olorun is served by a pantheon of lesser gods known as orishas. Each Orisha is associated with a particular aspect of human life, such as love, fertility, or war. Practitioners of Isese believe that it is possible to commune with the orishas and request their help in dealing with everyday problems.

Isese was brought to the Americas by Yoruba enslaved people who were taken to Brazil and Cuba during the Atlantic slave trade. In Cuba, the religion merged with Catholicism to create the popular Afro-Cuban religion of Santeria. In Brazil, Isese evolved into Candomblé, another Afro-Brazilian religion. Today, there are estimated to be over 100 million followers of Isese and its various offshoots around the world.

## Cultural and Historical Context

Isese is about spirituality, community, and culture. Isese practitioners believe that everyone has two sides to their personality and that it is crucial to balance these two sides to lead a happy and healthy life. To achieve this balance, Isese practitioners use a variety of techniques, including trance rituals, singing, dancing, and drumming. Isese is often practiced within community events and ceremonies, as it is believed that the community can support and heal individuals. The practice has a long history within Yoruba culture and continues to be a vital aspect of Yoruba identity today.

## Structure and Practice of Isese

The core tenets of Isese revolve around the worship of Olodumare, the supreme creator god, and the spirits known as Orisha. Adherents of Isese believe that Orisha occupies a realm between the human and divine worlds and serves as a mediator between Olodumare and humanity. Isese is typically practiced through communal rituals and ceremonies, often involving singing, dancing, and drumming. These activities promote a sense of community and unity amongst practitioners while also facilitating contact with the Orisha. Isese is a complex and dynamic belief system that millions of people have practiced for centuries.

# Becoming a Babalawo

In the Yoruba religion, a Babalawo is a priest who serves as a mediator between the human world and the spirit world. The role of the Babalawo is to perform rituals and offer guidance to those who seek it. Becoming a Babalawo is not an easy task. It requires years of study and apprenticeship under an experienced Babalawo. The first step is to complete a course of study at a Yoruba divinity school. This typically takes four years. Once you have completed your studies, you will be apprenticed to an experienced Babalawo for two years. During this apprenticeship, you'll learn how to perform rituals and interpret omens. After completing your apprenticeship, you'll be ready to take on the role of Babalawo yourself.

Babalawo act as mediators between the human and spirit world.
Creator:Dierk Lange, CC BY-SA 2.5 <https://creativecommons.org/licenses/by-sa/2.5/deed.en> via Wikimedia Commons https://commons.wikimedia.org/wiki/File:Obatala_Priester_im_Tempel.jpg

# Formal Initiation into Isese

Initiates into Isese undergo a rigorous process of study and training, which can last for many years. The final stage of initiation is a formal ceremony in which the initiate is formally recognized as a priest or priestess of the religion. The ceremony involves making offerings to the ancestors and nature spirits and is often followed by a feast. Initiates into

Isese are expected to maintain a strict code of conduct, and they are required to wear special clothing and jewelry that signifies their status within the religion. Initiates into Isese often find themselves at the center of their community, serving as spiritual leaders and counselors.

## Worship Practices of Isese

Isese practitioners believe in the power of ritual and ceremony to bring spiritual healing and balance. Here is a brief overview of the rituals and ceremonies that Isese practitioners typically perform:

### 1. Rites and Rituals

There are various rites and rituals associated with the religion of Yoruba. These are performed to promote balance and harmony in the world and honor the multiple deities of the religion. Some are performed communally, while others may be done individually. Common rites and rituals include offerings to the ancestors and nature spirits, chanting prayers, and making sacrifices. Many of these rites and rituals are still performed today and play an important role in the lives of those who practice Yoruba. From births and naming ceremonies to funerals and memorials, Isese helps Yoruba people to connect with their ancestors and the spirit world. It is a religion steeped in tradition and history, and its practices continue to provide comfort and strength to its followers.

### 2. Offerings and Sacrifices

The tradition of offering and sacrificing to the gods is an essential part of the Isese religion. Offerings can be anything from food and drink to candles and incense. Offerings are typically made in thanks for blessings or guidance, to seek protection from misfortune, and to honor the ancestors. Sacrifices, on the other hand, are usually more extreme. They may involve killing an animal. The purpose of a sacrifice is to show ultimate devotion to the gods and to receive their blessings. While some people may see these practices as barbaric, they are essential to the Isese religion.

### 3. Communing with Ancestors

Isese is based on the belief that the deceased continue to play an active role in the lives of their loved ones and that they can help to protect and guide them from the spirit world. Yoruba people often communicate with their ancestors through prayer, dance, and song. They also offer their ancestors food, water, and other items to honor them. In some cases, they will even ask their ancestors for advice or guidance on critical decisions. By maintaining a close connection with their ancestors, the Yoruba people can tap into a powerful source of wisdom and protection.

## Key Figures and Symbols of Isese

Isese is an Afro-Brazilian religion that originates from the Yoruba people of West Africa. Many of the key figures and symbols in Isese come from Yoruba mythology. For example, the Orisha Oshun is associated with rivers and fertility and is often represented by a yellow butterfly. Similarly, the Orisha Obatala is associated with wisdom and purity and is often represented by a white dove. Other important symbols in Isese include beads, feathers, and shells, which are used in rituals and ceremonies. Together, these key figures and symbols play an essential role in the practice of Isese.

### Isese vs. Traditional African Spirituality

Traditional African spirituality is based on the belief that everything in the universe is connected. This includes animals, plants, rocks, and even the spirits of the dead. God is seen as being present in all of creation, and humans are seen as part of this larger whole. As such, traditional African spirituality stresses the importance of living in harmony with the natural world. In contrast, Isese is a more individualistic religion that focuses on personal salvation and spiritual growth. While both religions have unique beliefs, they share a common goal: To help people lead fulfilled and meaningful lives. As such, they offer two different but equally valid paths to spiritual enlightenment.

### Differences between Isese and Other African Traditions

Isese is an African tradition that is unique in many ways. For one, it is the only African tradition that focuses on the role of ancestors in the lives of the living. In addition, it is one of the few traditions that still rely heavily on oral storytelling. Isese also strongly focuses on community, which is evident in how families and clans are organized. Finally, Isese is distinguished by its use of symbols and rituals to communicate significant cultural values. While Isese shares some similarities with other African traditions, its distinctive features help it to stand out from the crowd.

### Origin Stories and Practices

Many origin stories and practices are associated with the Isese tradition in Africa. In many other African traditions, ancestors are venerated and respected, but they are not necessarily seen as an integral part of everyday life. For the Isese people, however, ancestors are an essential part of their culture and play a role in everything from decision-making to healing. Another significant difference is the practice of divination. In Isese tradition, divination is used to communicate with spirits and seek guidance from them. This is a key part of their religious practice, and it is something that sets them apart from other African traditions.

### Symbology and Practice Structures

The study of symbology is crucial to understanding both Isese and other religious traditions from around the world. Isese is often said to be a "symbolic" religion, meaning it uses symbols to represent ideas or realities. This use of symbols is one example of how Isese differs from other religious traditions. In contrast to Isese, many other religions focus on practices rather than symbols. For example, Hinduism has a complex system of puja, or worship, while Buddhism emphasizes meditation and the Noble Eightfold Path. This focus on practices rather than symbols means that Isese can be seen as a more "experiential" religion, while other religions are more "conceptual." While there are important differences between these two approaches to religion, both Isese and other religious traditions offer valuable insights into the human experience.

## Essential Principles of Isese

The essential principles of Isese are based on the belief that humans can achieve spiritual growth and fulfillment through natural practices. This includes following a set of moral principles, such as respect for self and others, honoring ancestors, and living in harmony with the natural world. Here are some essential principles of Isese:

### Duality

Isese is a principle of Yoruba cosmology that holds that everything in the universe is composed of both spirit and matter. This duality is reflected in the fact that all humans have an Egungun, or ancestral spirit, and an Orixa, or guardian spirit. These two spirits are believed to work together to guide and protect the individual. In addition to providing strength and guidance, Isese teaches that all humans are connected to the natural world. This interconnectedness is reflected in the fact that humans are born with a destiny, or Orunmila, determined by their past actions. By understanding and following the principle of Isese, individuals can live in harmony with the natural world and fulfill their destinies.

### Ancestor Veneration

The practice of ancestor veneration is central to Isese, and it is thought to be one of the oldest religious traditions in the world. The Yoruba believe that the spirits of deceased ancestors continue to play an active role in the lives of their descendants. As such, they must be honored and respected through ritual offerings and prayers. In return, the ancestors bestow blessings upon their families and protect them from harm. This reciprocal relationship between the living and the dead is essential for maintaining balance and order in the universe. Without it, chaos would reign. Thus, ancestor veneration is a central principle of Isese and plays a vital role in upholding the cosmic order.

### Nature Worship

Practitioners believe that the natural world is imbued with creative power and that working in harmony with this power can bring about personal and communal transformation. As such, they pay reverence to a pantheon of deities who oversee different aspects of nature, including earth, wind, fire, and water. Isese followers also believe that humans are an integral part of nature and should therefore strive to live in balance with their surroundings. This manifests in their practice of using natural materials in their rituals and ceremonies and their focus on sustainable living. By honoring the natural world and our place within it, Isese practitioners hope to create a more just and equitable society.

### Divination and Healing

In the Yoruba tradition, there is a saying, "Ife ni mo pin, mo juba l'aiye," which means, "Ife is my tablet, I will erase it and start afresh in life." This saying encapsulates the essential principle of Isese, which is that through divination and healing, we can learn from our mistakes, make amends, and start afresh. The process of Isese helps us connect with our ancestors and the spirit world so that we can receive guidance and support on our journey. It is believed that when we let go of the past, we open ourselves up to new possibilities and potentials. Isese is, therefore, an essential principle for those who wish to create positive change in their lives.

### Understanding and Acceptance of Natural Cycles

Isese describes the interconnectedness of all things and the natural cycles of life. For example, we rely on the cycle of seasons to provide us with food and water. The cycle of day and night gives us a regular rhythm in our lives. And the cycle of birth, death, and rebirth is a reminder that life is ever-changing and always unfolding. Understanding and accepting these natural cycles allows us to live in harmony with the world around us. This principle of Isese is essential for achieving balance and peace in our lives.

### Commitment to Righteousness

Isese refers to the commitment to righteousness and truth and is often symbolized by the color white. To be pure in heart and mind is to be free from corruption and deceit, and those committed to Isese strive to live their lives by this principle. The pursuit of Isese is a lifelong journey, and it is believed that through Isese, one can attain spiritual enlightenment. In a world that is often filled with chaos and confusion, commitment to Isese can be a source of strength and guidance. For those who follow this path, Isese is more than just a religious practice; it is a way of life.

### Recognizing the Power of Words

In the Yoruba tradition, it is said that "ese" (pronounced eh-shay) is the greatest of all powers. This is because our words can create and destroy. They can heal or hurt, build up or tear down. That is why it is critical to be mindful of our words. Every word we speak has energy and power behind it. This is why we must always choose our words carefully. When we speak words of love, peace, and happiness, we are helping to create a more positive world. On the other hand, when we use negative words engendered by hate, anger, and violence, we are contributing to the problems in our world. This is a fundamental principle of Isese, which means "respect for all things" in Yoruba. By respecting the power of our words, we can help to create a more positive world for all.

## Tips for Pronouncing Yoruba Terms

Yoruba is a language spoken by the Yoruba people of West Africa. Here are a few tips for pronouncing some common Yoruba terms:

- Isese (pronounced: ee-shay-shay)
- Babalawo (pronounced: BAH-bah-lah-woh)
- Ifa (pronounced: ee-fah)
- Odu (pronounced: oh-doo)
- Orisha (pronounced: oh-REE-shah)
- Ebo (pronounced: eh-boh)
- Ase (pronounced: ah-shay)
- Iyanifa (pronounced: ee-yah-nee-fah)
- Iyanifara (pronounced: ee-yah-nee-fah-rah)

These are just a few examples of the many Yoruba terms you may encounter in this book. Learning to pronounce them correctly will help you understand the concepts presented in this book more accurately and fully.

As we have seen, Isese is an ancient tradition that provides us with a path to spiritual enlightenment. Through its core principles, we can live in harmony with the natural cycles of life, pursue righteousness and truth, and recognize the power of our words. By embracing Isese and employing its principles in our lives, we can create a more positive world for ourselves and for generations to come.

The next chapter will explore Olodumare, the Supreme Being, and other orishas in more detail. We will discuss their roles within the spiritual system of Isese and how practitioners worship them. We will also explore the creation story and examine this sacred divination system.

# Chapter 2: Olodumare, the Cosmos, and You

Olodumare, the Supreme One, is a powerful and compassionate deity in the Yoruba religion. For millennia, Olodumare has been worshiped for his immense power and is believed to be the Creator of all that exists in the physical realm (Aye). In Yoruba cosmology, Olodumare is the source of all life and is seen as a benevolent force that guides and protects humanity.

Olodumare is the ruler of the universe.
*https://unsplash.com/photos/Oze6U2m1oYU*

This chapter will explore the importance of Olodumare in the Yoruba spiritual concepts and cosmology, how he is depicted in nature, mythology, religious beliefs, art, and music, his characteristics, his role in Yoruba society, and the teachings associated with him. We will also look at Olodumare's relationship and influence with Obatala, the Creator's agent and emissary, and how Olodumare influences the physical realm (Aye). Finally, we will discuss the importance of respecting and thanking Olodumare in everyday life. By understanding Olodumare and his role in Yoruba spirituality, we can better appreciate the power and beauty of this ancient religion. Olodumare is more than just a divine being; he is an integral part of Yoruba spirituality, cosmology, and culture.

## Olodumare — The Supreme One

In the Yoruba religion, Olodumare is the Supreme One, the creator and ruler of the universe. Olodumare is often depicted as a young man, full of energy and life. He is said to be kind and loving but also just and fair. Olodumare is invoked in times of need, for example, when people seek guidance or strength. He is also associated with fertility and new beginnings. In many ways, Olodumare represents the best of what humanity can be: Creative, vibrant, and full of hope. Followers of the Yoruba religion believe that Olodumare is a guiding force in life, always there to provide guidance and protection.

## Depictions of Olodumare

In Yoruba mythology, Olodumare is usually depicted as a young man with a long beard, wearing a linen cloth around his waist. He is sometimes shown with four arms, holding a staff and a sword. In some traditions, he is also associated with the Sun and the color white. Olodumare is usually portrayed as a benevolent god concerned with the well-being of humanity. He is invoked in prayers for healing and guidance and is believed to be the source of all abundance and prosperity. In many ways, he embodies the highest ideal of what it means to be divine.

### A. In Nature

As mentioned, Olodumare is often depicted as the Sun, which makes sense given that he is the Yoruba god of creation. The Sun is a powerful symbol of life and growth, and it is easy to see how Olodumare might be associated with such an emblem. In some cultures, the Sun is also seen as a harbinger of death, so Olodumare's connection to it might be seen as a representation of the cyclical nature of life. Whatever the case, it's clear that Olodumare is a force to be reckoned with and that nature itself speaks to the power of this Yoruba deity.

Olodumare is depicted as the sun in nature.
*https://unsplash.com/photos/obsBswnv7FI*

### B. In Mythology

In Yoruba mythology, Olodumare is responsible for the orderly functioning of the universe. He is often portrayed as a wise and benevolent father figure who dispenses justice fairly and evenly. Many myths associate Olodumare with the Sun, depicting him as dousing the world in light and warmth. While he is typically shown as being kind and just, Olodumare is also capable of great wrath, and those who anger him can expect to suffer severe consequences. Ultimately, Olodumare is a powerful and merciful god who ensures the world runs smoothly.

### C. In Religious Beliefs

Olodumare is a supreme god in the Yoruba religion. He is depicted as the creator of the universe and the source of all life. Olodumare is also associated with rain and thunder. In some beliefs, he is said to live in the sky, while in others, he is seen as a more distant and mysterious figure. Regarded as a benevolent deity, he rewards those who follow his teachings and punishes those who go against him. His presence is often invoked in religious ceremonies and prayers, particularly when the

Yoruba people seek guidance or strength.

### D. In Art and Music

Olodumare is adorned with symbols of fertility. In music, Olodumare is represented by the drum, the instrument through which he communicates with the world. In art, Olodumare is portrayed as a peaceful and benevolent figure surrounded by animals and plants. In some artwork, he is shown as a powerful figure with four arms and a long beard. Olodumare's symbols of fertility and benevolence can be seen in many works of art throughout the Yoruban culture. For instance, some sculptures depict him as a guardian of nature and fertility, while others portray him as a wise and compassionate ruler.

## Characteristics of Olodumare

In the Yoruba religion, Olodumare is a source of wisdom and knowledge, and he is always available to help humans when they need guidance. Olodumare is also known for his sense of humor, and he enjoys making people laugh. In addition to being the creator god, Olodumare is responsible for maintaining order in the universe. He does this by ensuring that all beings follow the natural laws he has set forth. Olodumare is a powerful and central figure in the Yoruba religion and is revered by all who believe in him. Here are some characteristics of Olodumare that are important to note:

### A. Omnipotent

In the Yoruba religion, Olodumare is often described as omnipotent, meaning that he has the power to do anything. In addition to being all-powerful, Olodumare is all-knowing and all-seeing. He is the one who decides what happens in the world, and no one can escape his judgment. As the ultimate authority, Olodumare is invoked in times of trouble or danger. His power is absolute, and those who worship him believe he can protect them from harm. Whether you believe in Olodumare or not, there is no denying that he is a powerful force in Yoruba religion.

### B. Omniscient

In Yoruba mythology, Olodumare is omniscient, meaning he knows everything that has happened, is happening, and all that will happen. He is believed to live in the sky and communicates with humans through oracles. If you want to ask Olodumare a question, you must first go to an oracle who will relay your question to Olodumare. In return,

Olodumare will give the oracle a message to give to you. While Olodumare is kind and benevolent, he is also just and will not hesitate to punish those disobeying him. Followers believe that if they anger Olodumare, he may send thunder and lightning to destroy their crops or harm their livestock. For this reason, they always show respect for Olodumare and follow his commands.

### C. All-Loving and All-Forgiving

Olodumare is an all-loving god because he loves all his children equally. He does not love one more than the other. He loves all his children with the same love. Olodumare is also all-forgiving. If his children make mistakes, he forgives them. He does not hold grudges against them and loves his children unconditionally. He does not love them because they are good or behave in a certain way. He loves them no matter what they do or how they behave. Olodumare is also all-merciful. If his children are in pain or suffering, he has mercy on them and helps them.

## The Role of Olodumare in Yoruba Society

Olodumare is the creator god in the Yoruba religion who is responsible for everything that exists and controls the destiny of all humans. Olodumare is the source of all good things. In addition to being a powerful creator god, Olodumare is also seen as a guardian and protector. He watches over his people and is sometimes invoked in times of trouble or danger. Olodumare is a central figure in Yoruba society and plays an important role in the lives of all Yoruba people.

### A. As a Source of Guidance and Support

Olodumare is responsible for the ordering of the universe and is the ultimate source of guidance and support for humans. In Yoruba society, Olodumare is often invoked during times of need, such as when someone is having difficulty conceiving a child or crop yields are low. He is also thought to be the protector of orphans and widows. Olodumare is typically portrayed as a kind and benevolent god, and his worshipers often pray to him for guidance, protection, and prosperity.

### B. The Creator in Yoruba Religion and Cosmology

In Yoruba religion and cosmology, Olodumare is often called Olorun or Olofi. Olodumare is said to have created the world and everything in it, including humans, animals, plants, and the elements. He is also responsible for maintaining balance and harmony in the world. Olodumare is often portrayed as a kind and benevolent deity interested in the welfare of his creations. He is seen as a stern and just judge who punishes those who break the laws of nature. Regardless of how he is viewed, Olodumare is an important part of Yoruba religion and cosmology and plays a vital role in the lives of practitioners.

### C. Olodumare's Role in the Creation Story

The creation story of Olodumare is an important part of Yoruba cosmology. According to the myth, Olodumare created the universe and all living things. He used his breath to bring life into existence and endowed each creature with special gifts and abilities. Olodumare gave humans the power of intelligence and creativity, and he tasked them with caring for the world and all it contains. Olodumare also gave humans free will to make their own choices about how they will live their lives. In the end, Olodumare is seen as the ultimate source of all life and all creation. He is responsible for everything that exists in the physical realm.

# Olodumare and Obatala — The Creator and His Agent

Olodumare is the creator of all things, and Obatala is his agent. Olodumare is the source of all life, and Obatala is the one who brings it into being. Obatala shapes and molds the world, while Olodumare gives it form. Together, they are responsible for everything that exists. Olodumare is kind and loving, while Obatala is firm and just. They are both essential to the world and its inhabitants. We owe them both our thanks and our respect.

### A. Obatala as Olodumare's Emissary

In Yoruba mythology, Obatala is the God of Creativity and Orisha of calm waters. He is also known as the father of all orishas, as he was the first to descend from Olodumare's heavens to the earth. Obatala is often depicted as a wise and peaceful elder, and he is associated with purity, chastity, and peace. As Olodumare's emissary, Obatala brings peace and order to the world. He is responsible for creating human beings and infusing them with his essence of calmness and peace. In many ways, Obatala embodies all that is good and holy in the world. He is a powerful force for good, and his presence is always a welcome addition to any situation.

### B. The Significance of Obatala

Obatala is an important deity in the Yoruba religion. He is thought to be the patron of artists and healers, and his symbols include the colors white and silver. To many Yoruba people, Obatala is a powerful source of strength and inspiration. According to Yoruba belief, Obatala was the one who brought light and order to the world, and he is often invoked in prayers for peace and harmony. Obatala's role as Olodumare's emissary is important, and his presence in the world serves as a reminder of Olodumare's love and compassion for all living things.

### C. The Relationship between Olodumare and Obatala

In the Yoruba religion, Obatala is one of Olodumare's chief subordinates. Although Obatala is subordinate to Olodumare, the two have a close relationship. Olodumare often consults with Obatala when making decisions about human affairs, and Obatala is said to be Olodumare's favorite child. In turn, Obatala is very loyal to Olodumare and always strives to please him. This close relationship between Olodumare and Obatala is reflected in the many stories and legends about them in Yoruba tradition.

One such story is the myth of how Obatala created the world. According to this myth, Olodumare gave Obatala a white palm nut and told him to create the world from it. Obatala accepted this challenge, and with his great intelligence and creativity, he created the earth, the sky, the seas, and all of the creatures that inhabit them. Obatala then presented his creation to Olodumare, who praised him for his work.

This myth illustrates the close bond between Olodumare and Obatala and their respective roles in the creation of the universe. It also shows that while Obatala is subordinate to Olodumare, he still plays an important role in the divine hierarchy. Obatala is a source of creativity and order and a reminder of Olodumare's love and benevolence.

## Olodumare and the Physical Realm

Olodumare is a force of nature, and his energy can be seen in the ever-changing patterns of the world around us. Olodumare is responsible for guiding the destiny of humanity, and he is the source of all good and evil. While sometimes seen as a cruel god, he is also known to be just and fair, dispensing rewards and punishments according to our actions. In many ways, Olodumare represents the duality of life itself: He is both creator and destroyer, the giver and taker of life. It is through him that humans experience both joy and pain, success and failure. And it is only by understanding his will can humans can hope to achieve their goals in this world.

### The Connection between Olodumare and Aye

Although Olodumare is often considered distant and removed from the day-to-day affairs of humans, he is still very much connected and involved in the physical realm (Aye). In Yoruba belief, Olodumare constantly communicates with humans through various means such as dreams, visions, divination, and sacrifice. Understanding these messages from Olodumare allows humans to gain insight into their past, present, and future. Olodumare is also thought to be involved in creating each individual's fate, and through his guidance, a person can understand the cosmic order of the universe.

### Orishas as Emissaries of Olodumare

In addition to communicating with humans directly, Olodumare works through his emissaries, the orishas. The orishas are divine beings who act as intermediaries between Olodumare and humanity. Each orisha is associated with a specific area of life or energy and tasked with carrying out Olodumare's will in the physical realm. Through their guidance, humans can gain a better understanding of Olodumare's plans and have the opportunity to work toward their spiritual growth. The orishas act as divine guides, helping humans achieve harmony and balance in their lives.

## Teachings Associated with Olodumare

The teachings associated with Olodumare are varied and complex; however, a few core beliefs remain consistent. First and foremost, Olodumare teaches that all things are connected and interdependent and that all life is sacred. This includes the physical realm (Aye) and the spiritual realm (Ire). Olodumare also teaches that all beings have a purpose in life, and each person must strive to fulfill their destiny. Here are some other teachings that are often associated with Olodumare:

### A. The Need to Balance Opposites in Life

Olodumare teaches that to be successful, one must learn to balance the opposing forces of light and dark. This includes understanding how to constructively incorporate positive and negative energies into one's life . It also means recognizing the importance of order and chaos in the universe. With this understanding, one can strive to create a harmonious balance of energies in their life.

### B. The Importance of Respect and Gratitude

Olodumare encourages us to show respect and gratitude to the physical and spiritual realms. This includes showing appreciation for the cycles of nature and divine guidance that comes through dreams, visions, and divination. By demonstrating respect and gratitude for the divine forces at work, humans can learn to create a more harmonious balance within themselves. The importance of this respect and gratitude to Olodumare extends to our relationships with other people, as it helps us build more meaningful connections.

### C. The Power of Sacrifice

The Yoruba believe that Olodumare requires humans to make sacrifices to receive his divine guidance. Through sacrifice, humans exchange energy between the physical and spiritual realms. In this way, humans can understand the divine will of Olodumare and use it to improve their lives. The power of sacrifice brings a sense of gratitude and reverence that helps us connect with the divine. Sacrifices can be offered in the form of food, items, or even time and energy.

### D. The Need for Compassion and Mercy

Olodumare teaches us to be compassionate and merciful in our dealings with others. This includes understanding that everyone has their struggles and that we must be willing to show mercy and kindness even when someone has hurt us. By doing this, we can create a strong sense of harmony in our lives and the world around us. This can be difficult to grasp, but it is a powerful tool for understanding and connecting with the divine.

### E. The Role of Free Will and Responsibility

Olodumare believes that all humans have the power of free will; however, they must also take responsibility for their actions. This means recognizing the consequences of our choices and making the best decisions for ourselves and our communities. By exercising free will responsibly, we can move closer to achieving a spiritual balance in our lives and creating a more harmonious world.

Olodumare is the divine creator of the universe in the Yoruba religion. He is known as Olorun, Olofi, and Olofin. Olodumare is considered to be all-powerful, all-knowing, all-loving, and all-seeing. He is responsible for maintaining the balance of the universe and guiding the destiny of humanity. In addition to being the Supreme God, Olodumare is often associated with fertility and agriculture. Many of his worshippers offer prayers and sacrifices to him to ensure a good harvest.

Olodumare is sometimes invoked in healing rituals. He is believed to have the power to cure illness and restore health. Whether seeking guidance, protection, or healing, Olodumare is a powerful deity that can help you achieve your goals. The teachings of Olodumare provide an important foundation for understanding Yoruba spiritual beliefs and practices. These lessons are timeless, as they help us to connect with the divine, create meaningful relationships with others, and strive for a more balanced life.

By recognizing the power of sacrifice, respect, gratitude, compassion, mercy, free will, and responsibility, humans can strive to honor the divine.

# Chapter 3: Odu Ifa, the Divine Scripture

Most organized religions revolve around a holy literary corpus that encapsulates the religion's wisdom and experience, and Isese is no different. Isese is an earth-centered religion that believes in the interconnectedness of all things. The Yoruba people of Nigeria, Benin, and Togo are the custodians of this religion, and it is often passed down through their families. The Isese literary corpus includes the Ifa Corpus, which is a collection of stories, proverbs, and songs that teach moral lessons; the Odu Ifa Corpus, a set of sixteen sacred texts that guide everything from birth to death; and the Ogbe Ifa Corpus, a set of verses that are used in divination practices. Together, these three bodies of work form the foundation of the Isese religion and provide its followers with a rich source of wisdom and advice.

This chapter will provide an overview of the Odu Ifa Corpus, discussing its structure and content. We will also explore the major themes in Odu Ifa literature, summarize the texts, and explain their cultural and historical significance. Finally, we will discuss how Olodumare is thought to have created the Odu Ifa and what is involved in becoming a Babalawo, a highly-trained priest specializing in divination. At the end of this chapter, we will present the Sixteen Principles of Ifa, each with a brief explanation of its relevance and how to incorporate it into your life.

# Introduction and Overview of Odu Ifa

Odu Ifa is a Yoruba spiritual system used for divination and fortune-telling. The word "odu" means "sign" or "portent," and "ifa" means "Ifa Oracle." Odu Ifa is based on a body of sacred texts called the Ifa Corpus, which contains a wealth of information about the Yoruba people's history, cosmology, and mythology. Traditionally, Odu Ifa is encoded in a system of sixteen major signs, each corresponding to a different aspect of human life. The signs are often represented by cowrie shells, which are used in divination rituals. Odu Ifa is an essential part of Yoruba culture and plays a vital role in many people's lives in Nigeria and other countries with large Yoruba populations.

Cowrie Shells are used to represent the signs.
*https://pixnio.com/miscellaneous/seashell-mollusk-conch-gastropod#*

# Structure of the Odu Ifa Corpus

The Odu Ifa Corpus is a collection of over 2,300 poems in the Ifa divination system. The Corpus is divided into sixteen major sections; each is subdivided into numerous smaller sections. The first section, the Odu Ifa, contains most of the poems and is used for divining purposes. The other fifteen sections, the Esoteric Odu, are used for different purposes, such as initiations, sacrificial rituals, and prayers. The Corpus is also divided into two parts: The Exoteric Odu, which is available to all practitioners, and the Esoteric Odu, which is only available to those who have undergone initiation.

### A. Divination Verses

The Ifa literary Corpus is a collection of over 2,000 poems used in divination. The verses, known as Odu, are divided into sixteen main categories, each containing several sub-categories. There are 256 Odu used to interpret the signs and symbols that appear during a divination ceremony. While the Odu is primarily concerned with predicting the future, they also offer advice on everything from relationships to health and well-being. As such, they provide invaluable wisdom and guidance for those who consult the Ifa Oracle.

### B. Commentaries on the Verses

The Odu Ifa Corpus contains commentaries on the verses. These commentaries, known as Esoteric Odu, are composed of longer passages that explain and elaborate on the meaning of the verses. They provide further insight and guidance for those who consult the Ifa Oracle and reveal a great deal about Yoruba cosmology, mythology, and culture. The Esoteric Odu is primarily intended for those who have undergone initiation and are thus considered adepts or experts in the Ifa tradition.

### C. Other Texts

In addition to the Odu Ifa and Esoteric Odu, the Corpus also contains several other texts. These include hymns and prayers used in various rituals and stories about Yoruba gods, myths, and legends. The Corpus also includes information on the Yoruba people's history, customs, and beliefs. It is believed that Olodumare, the Creator God of the Yoruba people, created the Odu Ifa as a way for humans to understand the mysteries of life.

## Major Themes in Odu Ifa Literature

Odu Ifa is a body of religious literature concerned with the worship of the orishas—deities that control various aspects of human life. The Odu Ifa corpus includes myths, stories, and songs used in ceremonies and rituals. Many of these texts focus on the idea of harmonious living, emphasizing the need for humans to live in balance with nature. Other major themes include the importance of ancestors, the role of women in society, and the need to maintain a healthy mind and body. While some of these themes may seem timeless, they remain relevant today. As we strive to create a more just and sustainable world, the wisdom of Odu Ifa can help to guide our steps.

## A. Creation Stories

In the Odu Ifa texts, the Lord Ifa reveals himself as the creator of all things and speaks of his relationship with humanity. The Odu Ifa texts are divided into several categories: Creation stories, myths, folktales, and proverbs. Of these, the creation stories are perhaps the most important, as they offer insight into the Yoruba cosmology and worldview. In one popular creation story, the world is born from a cosmic egg hatched by a dove. From this egg emerge four beings, Obatala, Orisa-nla, Oduduwa, and Olorun. These beings go on to create everything else in the world, including humanity. While there are many versions of this story, all emphasize the importance of cooperation and interdependence in the world. As such, they provide an essential foundation for Yoruba culture and society.

## B. Deities and Supernatural Beings

In the Odu Ifa literature, many deities and supernatural beings play important roles. For example, Orunmila is the god of wisdom and divination, while Obatala is the god of peace and purity. Many other gods and goddesses preside over different aspects of human life. In addition to the gods, a variety of spirits, including the orishas, are responsible for guiding humans on their path in life. The Odu Ifa literature provides a wealth of information on these different beings and their roles in human life. As such, it is an essential resource for anyone interested in understanding the beliefs and traditions of the Yoruba people.

## C. Morality and Ethics

Odu Ifa contains a wealth of moral and ethical teachings. Traditionally recited by priests during religious ceremonies, these texts offer guidance on everything from the proper way to live one's life to the correct way to conduct business transactions. Many of the moral and ethical principles contained in Odu Ifa are still relevant today, and they offer a valuable perspective on how to live a virtuous life. The following are some of the most important moral and ethical teachings found in Odu Ifa:

- **Respecting Elders and Ancestors:** Odu Ifa teaches that respecting elders and ancestors is essential for maintaining social harmony. This principle is still relevant today, as

respecting elders is important to maintaining a cohesive society.
- **Honesty and Integrity:** Odu Ifa contains numerous tales about the importance of honesty and maintaining integrity. This principle is as important today as in ancient times, as honesty and integrity are essential for maintaining trust in any relationship.
- **Compassion:** One of the most prevalent themes in Odu Ifa is the importance of compassion. This virtue is essential for living a moral and ethical life, as it helps us to see the humanity in others and to treat them with kindness and respect.

### D. Rituals and Ceremonies

Many different types of rituals and ceremonies are described in the Odu Ifa literature. Some of these rituals are performed for particular purposes, such as healing the sick or asking for guidance from the spirits. Others are designed to be more general celebrations of life, love, and fertility. Regardless of their purpose, all of the rituals and ceremonies described in the Odu Ifa literature share a common goal: To bring people closer to the natural world and the gods living within it. By participating in these rituals, followers can learn to appreciate the rhythms of nature and better understand our place within the cosmos.

### E. Social Structures

In the West, we often think of literature as telling of an individual hero's journey. Works like the *Odyssey* or *Beowulf* are stories of individuals who, through their actions, come to define themselves and their place in society. However, in Odu Ifa literature, much focus is on social structures. Accounts of heroes are often used to illustrate the importance of family, friends, and community in achieving success. This emphasis on social structures can be seen as a reflection of the collectivist values of many African cultures. It also highlights that, in many cultures, an individual's identity is not solely determined by their actions but by those around them. As such, Odu Ifa literature provides a valuable window into the values and beliefs of African cultures.

### F. Proverbs, Wisdom, and Knowledge

Wisdom proverbs are an important part of Odu Ifa literature. These proverbs offer advice and guidance on various topics, from relationships to work to parenting. They are also often used to teach young people the significance of making good decisions. In addition to wisdom proverbs,

Odu Ifa literature contains a wealth of knowledge about the natural world, including information on animal behavior, plant life, and the Moon's cycles. This knowledge is essential for understanding the world and helping us make the best life choices.

## How Olodumare Created the Odu Ifa Corpus

Olodumare (also known as Olofi and Olorun) is said to be the creator of all things and is therefore believed to have created the Odu Ifa corpus. According to this belief, Olodumare used the power of his wisdom and divinity to create the Odu Ifa texts, which contain the answers to all questions and the solutions to all problems. The Odu Ifa corpus was written by the sixteen orishas, or Gods of Ifa, sent by Olodumare to impart his wisdom and knowledge to the people. The Ifa texts are seen as a direct link to Olodumare, and those who study them can learn the secrets of life from the god himself.

## Becoming a Babalawo and Learning the Texts

The Babalawo is the chief priest of Ifa and is responsible for interpreting the Odu Ifa, a sacred text that contains the wisdom of the Yoruba people. The Babalawo undergoes rigorous training to become qualified to interpret the Odu Ifa. After completing their training, Babalawos are considered experts in divination and Yoruba culture and play a crucial role in preserving traditional knowledge.

The Babalawo is trained rigorously to interpret the Odu Ifa.
Kehinde1234, CC BY-SA 4.0 <https://creativecommons.org/licenses/by-sa/4.0>, via Wikimedia Commons https://commons.wikimedia.org/wiki/File:Babalawo_Akinropo_(AKA._%E1%BB%8Cs%E1%BA%B9-tura_il%E1%BA%B9%CC%80_%C3%8Cb%C3%A0d%C3%A0n).jpg

## A. Initiation and Training

Followers of the Yoruba religion believe that humans are born with a connection to the orishas and that this connection can be strengthened through worship and ritual. One of the most important roles in the religion is that of the Babalawo, or priest. Babalawos undergo a lengthy process of initiation and training to become priests. The first step is to complete an apprenticeship under a senior Babalawo. During this time, the apprentice learns about the history and mythology of the Yoruba people and the traditional methods of divination. This typically takes several years, during which time the apprentice learns about the history and mythology of the Yoruba religion and its various rituals and ceremonies.

Once the apprenticeship is complete, the Babalawo undergoes a series of initiations to join the ranks of the priesthood. These initiations are designed to teach the Babalawo about the universe's energies and how to use them for divination. These trials are known as the "egungun," which test their knowledge and skills. Those who complete the egungun are considered to be fully qualified Babalawos.

## B. Learning the Verses and Commentaries

To become a Babalawo, one must first undergo extensive training in Ifa, the religion of the Yoruba people. This training typically takes place at an ile-Ifa, or house of Ifa, where a Babalawo-in-training will spend several years learning the verses and commentaries of Ifa. The Ifa corpus is vast and complex, and can take many years to master. However, the rewards of becoming a Babalawo are well worth the effort. As a Babalawo, a person can serve the community as a religious leader and counselor and have the opportunity to travel to Ifa shrines worldwide.

## C. Orisha Initiation Ceremonies

The initiation process to become a Babalawo is long and arduous; however, it is essential to understand the role and responsibilities of this important figure within the Yoruba religion. There are three main stages to the initiation process. The first is the Iwori Meji, which involves undergoing physical and spiritual tests. The second stage, Ikini Meji, requires the initiate to perform a series of rituals to purify their mind and body. Finally, during the Ogun Meji stage, the initiate undergoes a series of initiations that end with their formal induction into the role of Babalawo. Each stage of the process is critical in helping the initiate to understand the complexities of their new role and develop the skills needed to serve their community effectively.

## The Sixteen Principles of Ifa

At the root of the teachings and traditions of Ifa lies the Odu Ifa, a sacred text with over 256 verses that detail the laws of the universe and advice on how to live in harmony with God and creation. The Sixteen Principles of Ifa are fundamental principles derived from the Odu Ifa, which provide guidance and insight into Yoruban culture and religion. These principles are based on a deep understanding of how the universe works, and they can be used as a moral compass to help individuals strive for greater balance in their lives. The principles include:

1. **Omori** — Respect for the creator, Olodumare
2. **Iwa Pele** — The law of karma and balance
3. **Ore Oruko** — Respect for one's elders and ancestors
4. **Ebo Ri Aye** — Offerings in exchange for divine favor
5. **Ona Abiye** — Openness and honesty in dealing with others
6. **Oruko Akuko** — Honor for one's name and reputation
7. **Emi Ti Eja** — Care for the environment
8. **Se Iku Baba Wa** — Commitment to justice and fairness
9. **Onisowo Ni Iwa** — Respect for the rights of others
10. **Iwa Ni Ijinle** — Respect for tradition and knowledge
11. **Iwa Ni Imule Aye** — Respect for life
12. **Se Eru Igbeyawo** — Adherence to one's promises
13. **Omo Eniyan Lo Loju** — Kindness to others
14. **Iwa Ni Iwaju** — Respect for the law
15. **Se Ojuri Iwori** — Obedience to authority
16. **Alafia** — Peace, harmony, and well-being for all.

The Sixteen Principles of Ifa are essential teachings passed down through generations to uphold the sacred laws of Olodumare. These principles provide guidance and a code of conduct to live by and can be used as an ethical and moral compass to help individuals strive for greater balance in their lives. By following these principles, we can create more harmony, peace, and prosperity in our lives.

# Summary and Content of the Odu Ifa Texts

The first section of the Odu Ifa texts, the Odu Ifa, contains the story of the world's creation and the first humans.

The second section, the Ose Otura, contains the story of the god Oturanoia and his battle with the demon Olokun.

The third section, the Ose Irete, contains the story of the goddess Irete and her marriage to the god Orunmila.

The fourth section, the Ose Meji, contains the story of the twins Meji and their battle with disease.

The fifth section, the Ose Odi, contains the story of Odiraa and her journey to find her lost husband.

The sixth section, the Ose Obara, contains the story of Obara and his quest for power.

The seventh section, the Ose Ogunda, contains the story of Ogunda and his battle with death.

The eighth section, the Ose Osa, contains the story of Osa and her fight against evil.

The ninth section, the Ose Oturu, contains the story of Oturu and his journey to find himself.

The tenth section, the Ose Irete Ketu, contains Ketu's search for his lost wife.

The eleventh section, known as "12 oko temi eru pele pele l'owo ni iku ni osun meje ati ni agbara ni olorun ni iretitated- ifa," says that there should be twelve markets in every town so that people can trade goods and services, including food, medicine, clothes, shelter, metal works, woodwork, artifacts, jewelry, and tools.

The twelfth section, the Ose Oyeku, contains the story of Oyeku and his wisdom in dealing with a dispute between two villages.

The thirteenth section, the Odu Itefa, contains verses about Ifa divination and its power to predict the future accurately.

The fourteenth section, the Ose Ifa, contains verses of praise and reverence for Olodumare and guidance on living in harmony with nature and one's fellow man.

The fifteenth section, the Ose Odi Meji, contains verses dealing with social justice and staying true to one's values in the face of adversity.

The sixteenth section, the Ose Irete Akuaro, contains verses of worship for Olodumare and guidance on how to lead a life of righteousness.

The Odu Ifa Corpus is an essential source of knowledge and guidance for all followers of the Isese tradition. It contains a wealth of wisdom and insight into living in harmony with nature, our fellow humans, and ultimately with Olodumare. The Odu Ifa teaches how to make ethical decisions, stay true to one's values, and practice the teachings of Ifa. To become a Babalawo, one must learn at least a few verses from each Odu Ifa to gain knowledge and insight into each principle. Individuals can strive for greater balance and harmony by incorporating these principles into daily life.

# Chapter 4: Practicing Ifa Divination

The Odu Ifa, an ancient body of knowledge that contains all the secrets of life and holds extensive knowledge, is more than just a reference book. It is also the central element of the Ifa divination system. This Yoruba spiritual oracle helps individuals discover their destinies and plan their lives by these paths. It offers a practical way to help people who rely on natural laws, such as the law of cause and effect, achieve personal balance and wholeness. The Odu Ifa is not just a transactional tool; it can be seen as a manual for personal transformation!

Its documents provide useful insight into what makes us most true to ourselves, allowing us to embrace our greatness and foster purposeful relationships with ourselves, others, and nature to thrive. This chapter briefly introduces Ifa divination and its tools, symbols, and traditional practices. It also provides tips on interpreting these symbols and understanding the power of prayer. Finally, it includes information on how to access the guidance of Oracles and Babalawo.

## Introduction to Ifa Divination

Ifa divination is a traditional African system of divination based on the belief that a cosmic order governs human affairs. This order is known as Ashe, and it is believed to manifest in the patterns of nature. To access the Ashe, practitioners of Ifa use various methods, including tossing cowrie shells or other objects, to create patterns known as Odu. The

Odu are then interpreted to gain insight into the past, present, and future.

Ifa divination is often used for guidance in matters such as marriage, childbirth, business ventures, and other important life decisions. It is also used for healing purposes, both physical and spiritual. In recent years, Ifa has gained popularity outside its traditional home in West Africa, with practitioners now found worldwide. Whether you are seeking guidance or simply curious about this ancient divination system, Ifa offers a unique and powerful way to connect with the deeper forces at work in your life.

## A. History of Ifa Divination

The fascinating practice of Ifa divination has been a crucial part of African history for centuries. It is a form of divination using oracular chants and specific, sacred objects known as Opele. Many believe that these objects are used to divine the future. Practitioners all over Africa would use them and chants to attempt to answer all sorts of questions on behalf of their clients, from spiritual to personal matters. This holistic and compassionate practice has been adopted by many in recent years, primarily in Latin America and other regions with high populations of African descent. By furthering our understanding of Ifa divination's history, we can progress toward embracing its timeless wisdom.

## B. How Does It Work?

Ifa divination is an ancient system of divine guidance originating from the Yoruba people of West Africa. It is traditionally practiced by Adhafa, Ifa Priestesses, and Priests, who can communicate with the Orisha—the deities and spirits that occupy their world. The divination process begins with a consultation between the practitioner and the client. During this session, questions are asked about the client's life to determine what deities or energies influence them and how best to seek guidance for their situation.

The practitioner then uses a variety of sacred objects and symbols, such as cowrie shells or palm kernels, which reveal messages from the spiritual realm and provide advice, warnings, and predictions for future events or experiences. With its focus on inner transformation through connecting with one's energies, Ifa divination provides unique insight that can help bring clarity to situations and make positive changes in people's lives.

### C. Who Can Practice It

Practicing Ifa divination is an art form that can be studied and enhanced with dedication and the right guidance. Anyone open to learning the history and deep understanding of this African-based spiritual practice is capable of mastering it, regardless of gender, age, or cultural background. What sets Ifa divination apart from other forms of ancestral-based advice is its uniqueness in being a mental exercise—no tools are needed for practitioners to find answers and insight. With the proper respect and instruction from experienced teachers, all can become proficient in practicing Ifa divination.

## Tools Used in Ifa Divination

Ifa divination utilizes tools and objects to uncover knowledge and secrets about past, present, and future events. These tools include sixteen palm nuts and a chain or kola nut with eight dried janus cowrie shells attached. A diviner uses these tools to cast, throwing them onto a "divining tray" while they listen intently to the interpretation of the patterns made by where they land. Through this process, Ifa practitioners gain insight into how best to bring stability and balance into current situations or lives. It is believed that if one aligns themselves spiritually with the "cosmic force," one finds a sense of peace in life's difficulties.

### A. Divination Chain

The use of the Divination Chain (Opele) during Ifa divination is quite fascinating. This tool is composed of eight individually painted wooden blocks representing nature's forces and their influence on our lives. During a reading, they are cast onto an open palm or a conical diviner's tray to provide insight into difficult questions and situations. Each block within the divination chain is believed to carry a message from the Orisa, or spiritual realms, along with its associated energy. Through this divination process, we can gain clarity and guidance on all matters relating to our well-being and prosperity. It's no wonder that this ancient technique is so popular and potent today, as it has provided comfort and guidance for generations.

**Opele.**

*Dornicke, CC BY-SA 4.0 <https://creativecommons.org/licenses/by-sa/4.0>, via Wikimedia Commons https://commons.wikimedia.org/wiki/File:Opele_ifá%C3%A1_MN_01.jpg*

Opele is an important divination tool traditionally used to get answers to questions regarding a person's life, ranging from finding out why something is not working in their life to advice on upcoming business decisions. Opele consists of four sections, and Ifa priests or diviners perform the Opele divinations. As they divine, they make offerings and pray while shaking their Opele until it reveals their answer from the Orisha deities that provide guidance. Ultimately, it is believed that when asking Oshumare (meaning "divine messenger") for advice with this sacred tool, one can discover hidden truths about any given situation for greater understanding and progress.

### B. Cowrie Shells

Cowrie shells have an incredibly rich historical past concerning spiritual and divination practices, particularly Ifa Divination. Native to the Mediterranean, Persian Gulf, and parts of India, cowrie shells have been used as a form of currency by many cultures for many centuries. According to Ifa practitioners, cowries are believed to be messengers from the gods, helping with spiritual guidance and revelation. While Ifa divination alters between eight and sixteen pieces of these exquisitely smooth shells, they often come adorned with symbols and markings that can offer insight into the reading being conducted. They are a helpful tool for accessing knowledge from our ancestors, with their utilization offering us a connection to the Divine that is otherwise inaccessible.

### C. Palm Nut

The palm nut is an integral part of the Ifa Divination practice as it is a symbolic tool to communicate with and interpret the Orisa, spiritual energies. When performed, the Babalawo (divinity priest) will cast sixteen palm nuts in a traditional basket called ireke or ikin to receive messages from the divine. By deciphering how each nut has fallen, face down or upright, the Babalawo can determine which Orisha communicate through their blessings. And just like that, recommendations and advice will follow. This ancient tradition with an unbroken lineage of thousands of years is truly an incredible experience!

Palm Nut.
*Edithobayaa1, CC BY-SA 4.0 <https://creativecommons.org/licenses/by-sa/4.0>, via Wikimedia Commons https://commons.wikimedia.org/wiki/File:Palm_nut_in_Ghana.jpg*

### D. Ewe

Ewe, an African plant fiber, is an intrinsic part of Ifa Divination, a system of consulting oracles for spiritual guidance. Ewe is made from the inner bark of select species of trees, dried in the sun, and then rolled into thin strips. These little strips are a significant aid to divination by serving as a visual representation of fate and how it can be influenced through human intervention. The Ewe also reminds people to be mindful of their thoughts and words to remain aligned with their intention and manifest their desired outcomes. The power of the Ewe comes from its direct connection to the divine, allowing us to gain insight and guidance for any aspect of life.

### E. Ikin

Ikin is an ancient divination tool used in Ifa, a West African spiritual tradition. It is believed to connect people to the orishas, divine entities that can provide guidance and protection. Ikin is made of palm nuts, which are cast on a mat or sack to create patterns diviners interpret. The patterns created by the oracle give insight into current circumstances, obstacles, opportunities for the future, and advice on handling them. While knowledge of Ikin has become almost lost in recent years, it still offers an incredibly powerful way of gaining insight into our lives.

### F. Iroke

Iroke is an important tool used in Ifa divination. Iroke is a type of small to medium-sized sea snail that produces white and cream-colored shells, which are harvested for commercial use. These shells are believed to contain the spiritual energy necessary for diviners to communicate with the Yoruba orishas or gods. Used by Ifa priests and priestesses along with various other objects during divination ceremonies, Iroke can answer questions about health, employment, relationships, and more. Divination is an ancient practice used to bring harmony into people's lives. Ifa practitioners continue this tradition using Iroke shells today as they work with their clients to help them understand their challenges and find solutions within themselves.

## Odu Ifa Symbols

Odu Ifa symbols are an integral part of the Ifa religion, which is based on worshipping deities through encounters with divine messages or prophecies. These ancient symbols have been used for centuries and symbolize various aspects of Yoruba beliefs and traditions. Sixteen major

Odu Ifa sacred symbols represent many destinies, good and bad luck, wisdom and knowledge, protection from harm, fertility, well-being, success, and personal progress. All these help shape character behaviors among people who practice the traditional Yoruba faith. Each symbol has a unique meaning and provides its followers with spiritual guidance in their daily lives. Divination can be found in every path we walk in life, as these powerful symbols remind us to follow our destiny no matter how unpredictable it may seem!

### A. Meaning of Odu Ifa Symbols

Odu Ifa symbols are awe-inspiring relics of ancient African culture. Believed to be the narrations of millions of years ago, Odu Ifa is a sacred spiritual wisdom that provides insight into one's present and future. It is a corpus of symbolic verses culled from the timeless Orunmila, appointed by God as the custodian of knowledge, culture, and divination. Each symbol or Odu holds a unique meaning that can tell you about your destiny, relationships, guidance, and advice. There is power in knowing its secrets; it can help you make meaningful decisions and chart out a path for yourself in life. Unlocking these secrets is an exciting journey that offers untold wisdom.

| Eji-Ogbe | Oyeku Meji | Iwori Meji | Odi Meji | Ogunda Meji | Osa Meji | Oturupon Meji | Ika Meji |
|---|---|---|---|---|---|---|---|
| Irosun Meji | Owonrin Meji | Obara Meji | Okanran Meji | Otura Meji | Irete Meji | Ose Meji | Ofun Meji |

**Odu Ifa symbols.**

### B. Major Divination Circles

Odu Ifa is an oracle and system of divination that has been used for centuries to gain insight into a person's situations, relationships, and fate. The symbols represent words of guidance revealed in sixteen basic archetypes, often symbolically drawn with cowrie shells, palm nuts, or stones. A skilled interpreter of the Odu will study a configuration of these symbols to identify the one oracle it represents and provide detailed guidance from its particular foundation principles. Each symbol contains a stories related to past wisdom, symbolic characters with powerful stories, lessons in morality and conduct, and universal spiritual laws on the basis of which our experiences are created. Those with proficiency in Odu Ifa can offer insightful knowledge to those who seek it!

### C. Minor Divination Circles

Minor Divination Circles, or Odu Ifa Symbols, are essential to the African Yoruba culture. For centuries, they have been used to predict the future and offer advice on important life decisions. These symbols represent 256 different possible combinations or signposts that define the experiences of everyone's lives. They can be likened to GPS, guiding us down the paths we should take for the best outcomes. Every symbol has meaning, so those looking for insight into their present and future should familiarize themselves with them!

This form of divination originating in West Africa focuses on helping its patrons uncover deeper knowledge to understand the road ahead better. During this ritual, a recognized priest or initiate known as an Ifa Babalawo leads participants through a process that uses signs from shells or other objects to symbolize events and outcomes. Through this practice, individuals seeking guidance can gain direction on how to live their best lives and make informed decisions.

## Traditional Practices in Ifa Divination

The interpretation of Ifa divination requires a spiritual connection with the forces of nature and a keen understanding of Yoruba culture, language, and symbolism. The Babalawo or initiate must be trained and initiated in the necessary procedures to provide accurate interpretation. It is also important for them to understand the history and culture of each Odu and the relevant proverbs attached to them.

The traditional practice of Ifa divination involves using cowrie shells, or Opele, representing the signs of the 256 Odu. The Babalawo will cast these shells to determine what sign or Odu has been revealed and then offer advice according to the appropriate proverb. Additionally, other traditional tools, such as palm nuts and stones, may be used.

While its traditional practice requires a certain level of expertise, Ifa divination can also be practiced on a more basic level. Various books, tutorials, and websites online can help guide someone through the process of understanding each Odu and its meaning.

### A. The Written Word

The ancient practice of Ifa divination is based on the written word. As with many spiritual practices, a sacred language used in verbal and written readings establishes the foundation for divinatory wisdom. The written words used in Ifa divination are complex and in-depth, requiring special knowledge to interpret. Traditionally, an initiated priest or priestess partakes in the reading, often passing down the teachings to their apprentices over time. Today, online sources provide basic information to educate others on the foundational elements of this traditional method of divination. Although it is an ancient practice, it remains relevant today as a powerful spiritual guidance and transformation system.

### B. Poetry and Song

Ifa divination is at the core of the traditional Yoruba religion, with poetry and song being a crucial part of its practice. Through specially crafted verses, shamans or priests involved in Ifa divination can receive clarifying instructions from their gods about how to best navigate a variety of life's choices. Interesting and unique, these practices demonstrate the importance of strong literary origins within this ancient tradition. As its followers rely on orishas or deities for guidance, divining by poetic structure is especially meaningful to those whose culture has endured many generations. By contemplating their spiritual connection through the potent words of these poetic messages, the Ifa devotees emphasize an important aspect of the ritual practice as it holds the power to shape those who follow it positively.

### C. Oral Knowledge

While many practitioners today use written texts as aids, oral knowledge and traditional practices are still essential to this spiritual art. For example, every Ifa verse is chanted aloud to activate its power. It is a task that requires technical familiarity and emotional connection. Similarly, certain sacred songs accompanying divination readings must be sung in the original tonal language for the practice to be complete. This requires a skill that can only be acquired after dedicated study. As we seek new ways of understanding ourselves spiritually, it's essential not to underestimate the importance of traditional practices from cultures all over the world, such as those found within Ifa divination.

# Consulting the Oracles

Practitioners of Ifa divination have access to deep insight and wisdom through the ancient practice of consulting oracles. At its core, Ifa divination is an African spiritual tradition that embodies guidance and a conscious connection to ancestors, wherein practitioners connect with the Yoruba spirit-deities known as orishas for guidance. After a thorough incantation, one of 256 verses from an oracle called "Odu" is prayed over to gain spiritual insight. Through this type of divination, it is not just the current life that practitioners receive guidance on but also all realms in between this life and the next, a marvelous blessing that only genuine seekers can gain access to. By consulting the divine oracles within Ifa Divination, we invite lineage-speaking truth into our lives, enabling us to deeply explore difficult topics with real understanding and compassion.

## Tips for Interpreting Symbols

1. **Start with the basics:** Learn the meanings of each Odu and its corresponding symbols.
2. **Ask questions:** Contemplate what each symbol could mean about your current situation.
3. **Trust the process:** Follow your intuition and pay attention to signs that may provide further insight.
4. **Practice regularly:** Spend time exploring Ifa divination and its symbols to gain a deeper understanding of the practice.
5. **Seek guidance:** If you are serious about learning and practicing Ifa divination, seek assistance from a Babalawo or an initiated priest.
6. **Offering:** Before each reading, make an offering of thanks to the orishas for their help and guidance.
7. **Respect:** Approach each reading with respect and reverence, asking permission before attempting to interpret any symbols.
8. **Reflection:** After the reading is complete, reflect on what it could mean for your life.
9. **Gratitude:** Always thank the orishas and your ancestors for their guidance.
10. **Commitment:** Ifa divination is an ancient practice and should be approached with dedication.

Finding clarity through Ifa divination can give us deep insight into our lives and how to best move forward. Through the combination of written words, poetic songs, and traditional oral practices, the ancient art of Ifa divination offers powerful spiritual guidance for modern times. By educating ourselves and remaining open to the possibilities this practice offers, we can unlock a profound source of inner wisdom. With that, we can live our lives with greater understanding and joy.

# Chapter 5: The Seven Great Orishas

The orishas are divine entities that are thought to inhabit the Earth. They were worshiped in Africa before being brought over as part of the slave trade to the Americas. In Santeria, they are believed to be intermediaries between human beings and the supreme divine being, Olodumare. Santeria is an African-based religion that combines elements of the Yoruba and Roman Catholic faiths and is practiced in many countries, particularly in Latin America. Out of the multitude of orishas—some say that there are "400+1"—seven of them stand out due to their influence, power, and general popularity. These orishas are Elegua, Obatala, Oggun, Chango, Yemaya, Oshun, and Orunmila.

In this chapter, we will explore the characteristics and personalities of each of these orishas. We will discuss their domains, manifestations, stories, and holidays associated with them, as well as other correspondences such as colors, their preferred offerings, animals, and how to know if an Orisha is calling to you. Let us begin with a brief overview of the seven orishas. Later on, we will dive deeper into each one of them. By understanding their personalities and correspondences, we can better understand their roles in our lives and how to work with them.

# The Seven Orishas

The Yoruba religion of Nigeria is filled with many gods, goddesses, and other spiritual elements that make up its unique pantheon. Among the most important gods in this religion are the Seven Great Orishas, who serve as a foundation for many of the traditions and beliefs within Esese. These seven divine beings embody various aspects of the universe, such as air, storm, water, iron, fire, and fertility, granting their believers strength against misfortune. Adherents to Isese revere each of these orishas and often call upon them in times of need to intercede on their behalf. Through ceremonies and offerings to the orishas according to traditional customs and beliefs, practitioners can bring prosperity, luck, and protection into their lives.

## A. Elegua

Elegua, the Great Orisha, is a significant deity in the Yoruba religion. This power-filled deity presides over the intersections between heaven and earth, playing a role in bringing humans closer to the divine. While some may see Elegua as a chaotic figure with a mischievous streak, his real function is to balance the two realms of existence, from providing individuals with divine guidance to granting permission for personal and spiritual growth by opening doorways to success. His powers contain universal knowledge and unspoken secrets that can help individuals uncover their true purpose and destiny. As such, those who offer homage or initiate ritualistic offerings in his name are sure to have their prayers answered.

**Elegua.**
*Barbarella Gonzalez Acevedo, CC BY-SA 3.0 <https://creativecommons.org/licenses/by-sa/3.0>, via Wikimedia Commons*
*https://commons.wikimedia.org/wiki/File:Eleggua_TomasGonzalezPerez.jpg*

### B. Characteristics and Personality

Elegua is a powerful and unpredictable spirit. He is often depicted wearing red and black clothing, with his head covered by a hat or turban and a machete or staff in his hand. He is known for his sense of humor and being unafraid to speak his mind. He is also known to be a trickster and quite mischievous when it comes to getting what he wants; however, his intentions are usually good. He has a strong sense of justice and is a protector of the innocent, so he can be counted on to fight for those in need. Elegua is a strong believer in fate and destiny and works to ensure that everyone has their place on the path of life.

### C. Domains

Elegua is the gatekeeper and guardian of thresholds, portals, and doorways. He is responsible for opening the path to spiritual growth and providing protection and guidance on life's journey. He is also a protector of children and a guardian of fate and destiny.

### D. Manifestations

Elegua manifests in many forms, such as a small child, an old man, or a trickster. In his trickster form, he is often seen as a mischievous character who enjoys playing pranks on unsuspecting victims.

### E. Stories

Elegua is said to have been born from the union of two powerful orishas, Obatala and Yemaya. He is also known as the "owner of roads and pathways" because he is said to have created them. He is associated with fate and destiny and is known to be a powerful protector of children. He opened the doorways between heaven and earth so mortals could access to the divine.

### F. Associated Saint

The Catholic Saint of the Doorkeepers, Anthony of Padua, is often associated with Elegua. This connection is likely due to their shared role of opening pathways for spiritual growth. In some traditions, offerings to both Elegua and Saint Anthony are made to ensure spiritual protection.

### G. Holidays

The anniversary of Elegua's birth, Iku Osogbo, is celebrated in April. Elaborate ceremonies, offerings to Elegua, and communal feasts mark the holiday. The feast day of St. Anthony is celebrated on June 13, and followers of the Yoruba religion often offer prayers to him and Elegua on this day.

### H. Colors

Elegua is associated with red and black, representing his chaotic and unpredictable nature. He is also associated with white, symbolizing purity or innocence, and blue, representing the sea and his role as a guardian of portals between heaven and earth.

### I. Offerings

Elegua enjoys offerings such as cigars, rum, palm oil, and coconut. He likes sweet foods such as candy or fruits. Red and black are his colors, so offerings should be wrapped in these colors when possible. He also enjoys being praised with songs and stories.

### J. Animals

Animals associated with Elegua include monkeys, dogs, and roosters. These animals are seen as symbols of his mischievous nature and protectors of those who invoke his name. The rooster is a symbol of his connection to fate and destiny.

### K. Knowing if Elegua Is Calling You

If you feel Elegua is calling out to you, he may be. Look for signs such as imagery of Elegua in unexpected places or a sudden desire to learn more about him. He may appear in your dreams, offering messages or advice. Pay attention to your surroundings and any coincidences that may have a deeper meaning. If you feel Elegua is trying to communicate with you, be sure to listen.

Elegua always looks out for the best interests of his believers. He will provide guidance and protection on life's journey and bring success when prayed to properly. He may be unpredictable, but his intentions are always pure, and he will remain a powerful and revered orisha in Isese for centuries to come.

# Obatala

Obatala is one of the most important and powerful orishas in the Isese religion. Obatala is known as the Creator of Human Beings and the guardian of truth and justice. He carries a special machete to help him create humans from clay or cut away obstacles in our paths as we go about life. Obatala is associated with purity, light, white clothing, motherhood, and oysters. It is said that Obatala helped create Oyolu Meyi, charms worn for spiritual protection. We honor Obatala by celebrating the Obatala festival twice a year on December 22 and January

1. On these special days, people gather together in joyful festivities to give thanks to this great orisha for bestowing us with his divine protection!

### A. Characteristics and Personality

Obatala is known for his compassionate, wise, and just nature. He is a kind and loving orisha who values truth and justice. As the creator of human life, Obatala is deeply concerned with the welfare of humankind and will always be ready to offer guidance and protection. He's also known for his sense of justice and will always uphold fair judgment in any matter.

### B. Symbolism

Obatala is often represented by a white rooster, which symbolizes his power of creation, and is associated with the color white, which signifies purity and innocence. His machete symbolizes his power to cut away obstacles and create paths for his believers.

### C. Manifestations

Obatala is said to manifest himself as a white rooster or, in a dream, as an older man dressed in white. He is sometimes seen as a figure of light or an apparition of white smoke. Some may even hear his voice in their heads.

### D. Stories

There are several stories about Obatala and his connection to human life. One of the most well-known is the story of how he created humans out of clay. According to this story, Obatala crafted seven human bodies, each one unique and special, and brought them to life with the help of his machete. Another popular story is how Obatala created the world with the help of Orunmila, another powerful orisha. Together they crafted a perfect world, but the mischief of other orishas soon ruined it. To save his creation, Obatala sacrificed himself and underwent a great transformation, emerging as a white rooster.

### E. Associated Saint

Obatala is associated with Saint Michael, the Archangel. Both are protectors of justice and truth, and they carry a machete or sword as a symbol of their power. Obatala and Saint Michael are often invoked together in prayers to ensure protection and justice.

### F. Holidays and Festivals

The Obatala festival is celebrated twice a year on December 22 and January 1. During this festival, people come together to give thanks and honor this great orisha. Offerings are made, and people dance in his honor. Prayers are said for good health, protection, and prosperity. This is a time of joyous celebration in reverence to Obatala.

### G. Colors

The colors associated with Obatala are white and gold. White represents purity, innocence, and truth, while gold symbolizes wealth and prosperity. These colors are often seen in Obatala's clothing and decorations during festivals.

### H. Offerings

Obatala enjoys offerings such as white flowers, white clothes, sweets, and fruits. He also loves to receive oysters and other seafood as offerings. It is crucial always to give thanks and show respect when offering to Obatala.

### I. Animals

Obatala is associated with the white rooster, which symbolizes his power of creation. He is often seen riding a white horse in his chariot. He also has a special affinity for cats and is believed to look after them.

### J. Knowing if Obatala Is Calling You

If you feel a deep connection to Obatala, he is likely calling out to you. You may experience a feeling of peace and joy when you pray to him or visit his shrine. A strong sense of justice, truth, and compassion may be signs that Obatala is trying to reach out to you. If Obatala has called upon you, it is vital to answer his call and begin connecting with him.

Obatala's message to the world is one of justice, truth, and compassion. He's a protector and guide who helps us find our true purpose in life. His teachings teach us to break down obstacles, create paths, and reach our highest potential. It's essential to recognize Obatala's presence in our lives and be thankful for all he provides.

# Oggun

Oggun is a great power in Isese, the traditional spirituality of the Yoruba people's ethnicity and diaspora. Regarded as a maker of a brave and tempered character, wisdom, and strength, Oggun is one of the most popular orishas amongst those who practice Isese. Oggun is credited with giving success to human endeavors and providing magical protection for his devotees. He is an influential figure in ceremonies throughout Isese traditions, and his unique attributes cannot be overlooked by anyone who knows of him. Even if you have never encountered Oggun, there are many ways to learn more about him and connect with his teachings. For example, prayer or meditation can help you gain insight into this great orisha's strengths and potential. By understanding Ogun's mythology better and standing true to its teachings, you may find that encountering him can be an incredibly rewarding journey!

### A. Characteristics and Personality

Oggun is a powerful and courageous orisha who stands as a protector of justice. He has an intense personality, often seen as impatient and irritable. Oggun is quick to anger and often speaks his mind without fear of consequences. He fights for what he believes in and is loyal to his loved ones. Despite his temperamental nature, Oggun is also an incredibly generous orisha who will always lend a helping hand if asked. He is honest and direct but also kind-hearted and forgiving.

### B. Domain

Oggun is the orisha of war, labor, and iron. He works hard to ensure justice is served and that people are treated fairly. He is also the patron of artisans and blacksmiths, who are seen as his children. Oggun is often depicted carrying a machete, axe, or hammer. He is a master of all trades and can tackle any task put before him.

### C. Manifestations

Oggun is often represented in cabildos, or spiritual assemblies, as an old man with a white beard wearing blue clothing. He is also seen as a blacksmith or warrior, wielding an axe or machete. He can manifest himself as a bull, symbolizing his strength and courage. In some traditions, Oggun is also known to manifest as a hunter or fisherman.

### D. Stories

In Yoruba mythology, it is said that Oggun was born from the union of Obatala and Yemaya. His primary role was to protect humans from danger and conquer adversity. Oggun is a powerful warrior, fighting for justice and protecting the defenseless. In the famous story of Oggun and Osain, Oggun uses his machete to clear a path for an oppressed village to bring justice.

### E. Associated Saint

Oggun is associated with Saint Peter, the apostle of Jesus. Just like Oggun, St Peter is seen as a brave warrior who is strong in his faith and willing to fight for what he believes in. He is also a patron saint of fishermen, making him a perfect fit for Oggun.

### F. Holidays

Every year on June 29, devotees of Oggun celebrate his feast day with a great festival. The celebration usually includes an offering to Oggun and a ritual dance called the Opele. This day is seen as a time to honor Oggun and ask for his protection. Many regional traditions and festivals throughout the year celebrate different aspects of Oggun's power.

### G. Colors

The colors associated with Oggun are blue and white. Blue symbolizes his strength, courage, and perseverance. White stands for justice and purity. Oggun's colors are often used in ceremonies, offerings, and devotional items to honor him.

### H. Offerings

Regarding offerings, Oggun enjoys rum, cigars, and black coffee. He likes fruits, such as bananas and oranges, and offerings of iron and tools. Other items that can be used to honor Oggun include white candles, crosses, rosaries, and animal sacrifices. Any offerings made to Oggun must be done with the utmost respect and reverence.

### I. Animals

The animals associated with Oggun are bulls and horses. Bulls symbolize his strength, courage, and perseverance. Horses represent freedom and swiftness. Animals can be sacrificed to Oggun or used in rituals to honor him and ask for his protection.

### J. Knowing if Oggun Is Calling

When Oggun is calling, he will often manifest in dreams or visions. He can also be recognized by his colors, blue and white, or by the sound of a thunderclap. It is said that when he wants to communicate with his devotees, he will do so through metal objects such as nails, screws, or keys. If Oggun is calling, be respectful and answer his call with the appropriate offerings.

Oggun is a powerful and important Orisha who is worthy of respect. He works hard to uphold justice and protect the defenseless. Knowing more about Oggun and honoring him with offerings and rituals can help bring balance and harmony into our lives.

# Chango

Chango is a beloved orisha, or deity, in the traditional Isese religion found in Nigeria and other parts of West Africa. He is praised for being strong, swift, and confident, attributes treasured in the culture. Chango's responsibilities include protection from harm and illness as well as guidance through difficult times. His appreciation is expressed through elaborate festivals wherein his followers offer sacrifices, music, and dance to show their devotion and admiration. He is especially fond of Yoruba drumming music, so naturally, these gatherings are loud, vibrant, and joyous occasions that leave all involved feeling blessed after honoring this important spirit.

### A. Characteristics and Personality

Chango is often depicted as a male warrior with strong and muscular features. He is known for his strength, confidence, bravery, and battle and warfare skills. He's a passionate spirit who loves life, and his enthusiasm can be contagious. He's generous and compassionate, a natural leader who will stand up and fight for what is right. He has a temper, though, so it is best not to anger him.

### B. Domain

Chango is the orisha of thunder and lightning, war, fire, and justice. He has dominion over the physical and spiritual realms, so his influence is far-reaching. He is a patron of music, dance, poetry, blacksmiths, and metalsmiths. His power is often expressed through thunderstorms, which signify his presence.

### C. Manifestations

Chango manifests as a tall and powerful male figure dressed in red and crowned with an elaborate headdress of feathers. He is often seen carrying two swords, a machete, and an axe. A white dog or horse might also accompany him. When he is manifested in thunderstorms, he is accompanied by flashes of lightning and loud claps of thunder.

### D. Stories

In Yoruba mythology, Chango is said to be the son of Obatala and Yemaya, two important orishas in the traditional Isese religion. He is often portrayed as a brave warrior who fought to protect his people from harm and injustice. He was a great leader and teacher, guiding his people with wisdom and strength. He was also a great lover, marrying many wives throughout his life.

### E. Associated Saint

Chango is strongly associated with Saint Barbara, a Christian saint known for her faith and courage in the face of adversity. Her story serves as a reminder of Chango's power and protection, and she is often venerated alongside him in traditional ceremonies.

### F. Holidays

Chango's festivals are usually held in the summer months, during the hottest days of the year. During these celebrations, his devotees dress in red, the color of passion and strength, and offer sacrifices to him. The festivities are marked by drumming, dancing, and feasting. At the end of the festivities, Chango is thanked and praised for his protection.

### G. Colors

Chango's colors are red, white, and black. Red is a sign of his strength and courage, while white signifies purity and holiness. Black is associated with his power and ability to overcome adversity. These colors are often seen in Chango's traditional clothing and are used in offerings to him.

### H. Offerings

Chango's traditional offerings include red wine, rum, cigars, and roasted corn. He loves music, so offerings of drums, flutes, and other instruments are often given in his honor. Offerings of food, especially roasted chickens, are also appreciated. Other items associated with Chango include weapons, tools, jewelry, and books.

### I. Animals

Chango is associated with several animals, the most important being the white horse. This symbolizes courage and strength in battle and is used to honor Chango in ceremonies and festivals. The white dog is also associated with him, as it symbolizes loyalty and protection. Other animals include the cow, goat, and rooster.

### J. Knowing if Chango is Calling

When Chango is calling, you may feel a sudden surge of energy or see flashes of lightning. You may also find yourself drawn to the color red or feel a strong connection to the thunder and lightning. If you are feeling inspired, creative, brave, or confident, it could be a sign that Chango is calling you. Additionally, if you feel a sudden urge to take action or speak up for what is right, it could indicate that Chango is trying to get your attention. In any case, if you feel the presence of Chango and wish to honor him, it is best to make an offering and thank him for his protection.

The power of Chango is immense and should be respected. He is a source of strength and courage, inspiring his followers to stand up for what is right and fight injustice. When called upon, Chango is a formidable ally and protector. Make sure to honor him with offerings and thank him for his protection.

# Yemaya

Yemaya is a goddess within the ancient African religion of Isese. She is seen as the mother of all living things and governs acts of kindness, prosperity, and fertility. With her association with the Moon, Yemaya is known to be a kind spirit who provides positive balance in every situation. Legends say that no matter how bad the circumstance may be, she will always bring love and mercy. Many people invoke Yemaya to bring good fortune into their lives and increase their odds of success in all they do. Those who strongly believe in her powers are sure that wherever darkness may come, Yemaya will keep them safe and offer guidance during adversity. It is no wonder that she remains so beloved amongst her many devotees!

### A. Characteristics and Personality

Yemaya is a goddess of love and mercy, and her presence is often felt in moments of need, joy, or sorrow. She embodies hope and comfort and is a protector of children and those in need. She will often lend her assistance to those who call upon her. A common theme in Yemaya's personality is that of abundance and fertility. She is associated with the ocean and has been known to bring wealth as well as fertility. Yemaya is believed to have a strong connection to the Moon, and her influence is often seen in matters of emotions, intuition, and spiritual development.

### B. Domain

Yemaya is the ruler of the ocean and protector of all things that dwell within it. Her power can be felt on both land and sea, and she is known for protecting sailors, fishermen, and all who travel by water. The ocean also symbolizes fertility and abundance, and Yemaya is the perfect representation of this.

### C. Manifestations

Yemaya is often depicted as a mermaid, and she can be seen wearing jewelry made of shells and pearls. Her colors are blue and white, which are also associated with water and the ocean. She is often depicted with seven orbs or stones in her hands, symbolizing wealth, fertility, and abundance.

### D. Stories

One of the most famous stories about Yemaya is that she was born to Olokun, the father of all gods. It was said that Olokun had been looking out over the ocean one day when he saw a beautiful woman swimming in its depths. This woman was Yemaya, and she quickly became his favorite goddess. Yemaya was renowned for her kindness, generosity, and protection of those in need, and she always granted the wishes of her devotees. No matter how difficult the situation, Yemaya could be counted on for guidance and protection.

### E. Associated Saint

Yemaya has been associated with Saint Barbara, a Christian martyr who was killed for her faith. She is often seen as a protector of those who need guidance and strength during difficult times. St Barbara is often depicted holding a tower, symbolizing the protection she offers, or with a crown of pearls, representing Yemaya's domain of the ocean.

### F. Holidays

Many festivals celebrate Yemaya, but the most popular is the Yemaya Festival, which takes place on December 8. This festival is a time to give thanks to Yemaya for her protection and guidance and to ask for her assistance in the coming year. Yemaya devotees celebrate her birthday on August 15, known as "Yemaya Day."

### G. Colors

The colors that are most associated with Yemaya are blue and white. These colors represent the ocean and water, which is her domain. She is also often associated with the colors green and gold, representing fertility and abundance. Symbols such as shells, pearls, and seven stones are also associated with Yemaya.

### H. Offerings

Devotees of Yemaya often make offerings to her in the form of food, jewelry, or special items. These offerings are meant to show gratitude for her protection and guidance and can be placed on an altar dedicated to the goddess. Offerings can also be made during the Yemaya Festival or on any other special occasion which calls for thanks to be given to Yemaya.

### I. Animals

The animals most associated with Yemaya are dolphins and fish. Dolphins are often seen as a symbol of protection, while fish represent abundance and fertility. Yemaya is also associated with birds, especially peacocks, seagulls, and sea turtles, representing freedom and new beginnings.

### J. Knowing if Yemaya Is Calling

If you feel a strong connection to the ocean and if your intuition is particularly strong, or if you are seeking guidance for an important decision, Yemaya may be reaching out to you. Signs of her presence can include finding shells or dolphins as if by chance or even experiencing an unusual urge to take a boat ride. By paying attention to these signs and connecting with Yemaya, you can receive her gifts of guidance and protection.

The goddess Yemaya is a powerful and benevolent spirit of the sea. She is a protector and guide who offers strength and guidance to those in need. By understanding and connecting with Yemaya's energies, you can receive her gifts of protection, abundance, fertility, and freedom.

# Oshun

Goddess Oshun is a great orisha in Isese. She is understood and corresponded with through her many attributes, such as fertility, joy, and sensuality. Oshun is seen as a compassionate and generous deity and represents the creative force of the universe, flowing like the rivers she is frequently associated with. Many worshippers believe that she helps to restore balance and peace when one has strayed from their purpose or destiny in life. As an influential figure in African diasporic religious practice, Oshun is celebrated amongst communities around the world for her wisdom, love, and grace.

### A. Characteristics and Personality

Oshun is characterized as a powerful, loving, and nurturing mother figure. She is often seen as an embodiment of beauty, creativity, and fertility, a source of inspiration and hope, a powerful mediator between the spiritual and physical realms, and an essential protector of those she loves. This deity is known for her warm, inviting nature and often encourages people to embrace their vulnerabilities as a source of strength and power.

### B. Domain

Oshun is associated with the elements of water and air. Her domain includes rivers, lakes, oceans, and other sources of water. She is a source of life-giving energy, and her presence can be felt in the changing of the seasons or the ebb and flow of a river or stream. She's also seen as a protector of travelers and explorers, ensuring they reach their destination safely.

### C. Manifestations

Oshun is represented by a wide range of symbols and manifestations, including shells, fans, gold jewelry, peacock feathers, honey, and water lilies. She is often depicted with two or three strands of hair, wearing yellow or gold clothing, or with a crown of jewels. Her colors are typically bright and cheery, such as yellow and orange, and her number is five.

### D. Stories

Oshun is featured in many stories and lore across West African religions. One such story tells of how Oshun used her power to bring the dead back to life. Another story tells of how Oshun saved a village from famine by using her power over the rivers and oceans to bring an abundance of fish. Oshun is also known for her temper and can be vengeful when those she loves are wronged.

### E. Associated Saint

Saint Teresa of Ávila is often associated with Oshun due to her strong devotion to the Catholic faith and her love of nature. St. Teresa is a powerful and passionate advocate for the poor and vulnerable, and many believe she carries some of Oshun's energy. St. Teresa is also considered a patron saint of travel, as she often went on long journeys to preach and spread the faith.

### F. Holidays

Many African diasporic communities celebrate the holiday of Oshun every year, usually around August. This celebration is meant to honor and recognize the powerful presence of this Orisha and to be thankful for her many gifts. During Oshun's holiday, people usually celebrate with dancing, singing, and offerings of food, flowers, and other items.

Additionally, many people will take a boat ride to connect with the spirit of Oshun and ask for her blessings.

### G. Colors

The colors associated with Oshun are typically bright and cheerful, such as yellow and orange. These colors symbolize the energy of life and renewal that she brings, abundance, and joy. Gold and silver are also associated with Oshun, representing her power and wisdom. Additionally, Oshun is often depicted with a crown of jewels or other brightly colored items.

### H. Offerings

Oshun is usually offered food, flowers, and other items to honor her presence. Honey and fruits, coins, and jewelry are popular offerings associated with Oshun. Some people leave her offerings of music or dance to show their appreciation for all she has done. Additionally, Oshun is offered prayers and petitions for her blessings and guidance.

### I. Animals

The most common animals associated with Oshun are birds, particularly peacocks. Peacocks are seen as symbols of renewal and transformation, and they are often used to represent the energy of Oshun. Other animals associated with her include fish, frogs, and turtles, all of which symbolize abundance, protection, and fertility.

### J. Knowing if Oshun Is Calling

One of the most common signs that Oshun is calling can be found in nature. If you find yourself being drawn to a certain body of water or the beauty of a flower or tree, this could be a sign that Oshun is reaching out to you. Additionally, if you feel overwhelming joy, love, or abundance, this could be a sign that Oshun is near. Finally, if you have a strong sense of intuition, this could indicate that Oshun is calling.

# Orunmila

He is the all-knowing "Great Orisha," or spirit of divinity, in Isese. Orunmila is considered the true originator of the teachings of Ifa, which form the basis for morality within Yoruba spiritual belief. From these teachings, we learn how to live life in a balanced and harmonious manner and develop positive relationships with others and our natural environment. As such, Orunmila is often invoked during important ceremonies and rituals within West African society. He is also a great source of encouragement and solace during times of adversity by providing insight and guidance on creating a better future based on goodwill and hope. In this way, he has become an invaluable pillar of strength within Isese traditional culture and will never be forgotten or taken for granted!

### A. Characteristics and Personality

Orunmila is an intelligent, wise, and compassionate spirit. He is known for his ability to foresee the future, provide guidance on navigating the intricacies of life, be fair and just, and deal out punishments and rewards with a balanced hand. Additionally, Orunmila is seen as a protector of the weak and vulnerable, coming to their aid in times of need.

### B. Domain

Orunmila is closely associated with wisdom, knowledge, and understanding. He is often invoked for help in making important decisions or resolving disputes. Additionally, he's a great source of support and comfort in times of hardship and loss.

### C. Manifestations

Orunmila is often depicted as a wise older man dressed in traditional West African garb. He is sometimes shown with four eyes to symbolize his all-seeing wisdom and knowledge and sometimes depicted with a staff in one hand, symbolizing his power and authority.

### D. Stories

Orunmila is most commonly known as the storyteller who passes on the teachings of Ifa to others. He is also credited with the invention of the divination system, which is used to interpret messages from the gods and ancestors. Additionally, he's a great teacher and healer, using his wisdom to bring clarity and peace of mind to any situation. The symbol most associated with Orunmila is the staff, which he holds in his hand to signify his power and authority.

### E. Associated Saint

Saint Vincent de Paul, an influential seventeenth-century French priest and theologian who dedicated his life to helping the poor and marginalized, is the Catholic saint associated with Orunmila. He was known for his compassion, humility, and wise counsel, traits that Orunmila also embodies. He is a powerful example of how we can use our skills, knowledge, and understanding to bring about positive change in the world.

### F. Holidays

Orunmila is celebrated on the second day of the annual Ifa festival, which takes place in western Nigeria. On this day, people gather in public plazas to honor the spirit of Orunmila with songs, dances, and offerings. It is a day devoted to understanding and appreciating the teachings of Ifa and the power of knowledge.

### G. Colors

The colors associated with Orunmila include blue and white, representing his power and authority. Additionally, he is often depicted wearing a long white robe, symbolizing his wisdom and understanding. The colors remind us that we should strive to learn and grow in knowledge, just as Orunmila did.

### H. Offerings

Orunmila is often honored with offerings of sweet drinks, fruits, and other edible items. He accepts the offering of prayer and incense. Some people may give him a special gift or ritual object as a sign of their gratitude and appreciation for his wisdom and guidance.

### I. Animals

Orunmila is closely associated with the bird, symbolizing joy, freedom, and heavenly power. The dove is also a popular choice as an animal offering to Orunmila because of its symbolic meaning. Others may honor him with other animals, such as a goat, sheep, or dog.

### J. Knowing if Orunmila Is Calling

When Orunmila is calling, it can be a powerful experience. Signs that he may be calling you include feeling an inexplicable sense of peace and well-being, having strong dreams or visions, or hearing spiritual wisdom in your head. Additionally, it is said that when Orunmila calls a person, they will feel it in their heart. If these signs are present, it may be time to seek Orunmila's guidance.

Orunmila is an important figure in Yorùbá culture, as he is seen as a source of wisdom and guidance. His teachings, through the divination system, have helped many people make critical decisions or resolve conflicts. Additionally, his presence is felt in many West African countries, where he is celebrated for his powerful influence. By understanding the symbols associated with Orunmila, we can gain insight into his teachings and use them in our lives.

The Seven Great Orishas are essential figures in Yoruba culture. These spiritual leaders represent a variety of forces in nature, and each one brings its gifts to humanity. Elegua, Yemaya, Ogun, Oshun, Obatala, Shango, and Orunmila are all important figures in the Yoruba belief system, and understanding their symbols and stories can help us appreciate the power of their teachings.

By learning from these orishas, we can gain insight into how to live our lives with greater purpose, understanding, and respect for the world around us. We can also use their teachings to help guide our decisions and find balance in life. Understanding the symbols and stories associated with these orishas can be a powerful way to connect with their wisdom and guidance.

# Chapter 6: Walk the Path of Your Ancestors

Ancestral veneration, known as Isese, is integral to the Yoruba tradition. The term Egungun is used to describe Yoruba ancestors, and it holds great significance in Isese. Egungun encompasses respect for those who have passed and is a way of connecting with the orishas or deities. Understanding the different categories of ancestors and how to identify them is essential to appreciate the concept of Egungun fully. This chapter will discuss the importance of Egungun in Isese culture by exploring its definition, necessary traits for veneration, and categories of ancestors. Tips and rituals to identify ancestors will be explored, and we will conclude with a summary of the concept and importance of Egungun.

## The Concept of Egungun

Ancestors and ancestral veneration are two very important elements in the religion of Isese. Ancestors influence one's life and are seen as a bridge between humans and the orishas. It is customary for these ancestors to be written down on a patronage list. This list consists of names of deceased family members that were considered to have passed with good fortune and vitality. These ancestors are believed to be the gatekeepers into divine blessings from the orishas, so they need to be honored and respected through prayer and offerings.

In cases where a list cannot be created, Iyabó would serve as an ancestor, which is an individual divinity that looks out for the living but also remains connected in spirit to those who have died. Ultimately, paying homage to ancestral spirits can greatly help bring positive Gugbo (protection) over your living kin. A strong relationship between humans, deities, and those gone before us must constantly remain in balance so things go well here on Earth.

### A. Definition

Egungun is an important concept in Isese spirituality, which refers to ancestral spirits. These spirits connect with their descendants, and many rituals and ceremonies are conducted to create this connection. Egungun ceremonies involve colorful costumes, music, dance, and offerings. Many believe that the energetic release of these festivities helps the living and the dead come together in a shared spiritual experience. Through the Egungun rituals, those who have passed on continue to shape and influence the lives of their descendants in a very meaningful way.

### B. Respect and Veneration

These ancestors are revered for the good they have done, their strength, and the wisdom they provide to those still living. They are seen as gatekeepers who protect their living relatives from harm and guide them through difficult times. It is crucial to respect the wishes of these ancestors and pay homage to them to receive their blessings. The most meaningful way to show respect is by offering food and other items traditionally used in rituals during their lifetime.

### C. Long and Moral Life

To be an appropriate ancestor for veneration and respect, one must have lived a long and moral life. This means they have led a life of good character and done many great things to benefit their descendants. Ancestors who have passed away with a legacy of wisdom, honor, and strength are most likely to be venerated. To be considered an ancestor, one must have left behind a meaningful impression in the hearts and minds of their descendants. With the help of the gods, these ancestors are believed to pass on their wisdom and strength from the afterlife.

### D. Necessary Traits

The qualities of an ancestor are important to consider when determining who can be venerated. These traits include leadership, strength, humility, generosity, patience, understanding, and wisdom. Additionally, the ancestor must have passed away peacefully and not due to violence or accident. If these traits are met, the ancestor is believed to be a spiritual source of power and guidance for their descendants.

### E. Significance of Ancestors

Ancestors are seen as a bridge between humans and the orishas. This is because they are believed to bring blessings and protection to their living descendants in the form of Gugbo. Ancestors are seen as spiritual guides who can help guide their living family members through difficult times. It is said that paying homage to them can help ensure a long and prosperous life for their descendants and a positive future for their family line. Ultimately, honoring and respecting these ancestors is essential to maintaining balance and harmony in the world.

## Categories of Ancestors

Isese is built upon the family system with ancestors at its core. As part of the cultural heritage that ties individuals to their past and community, one must acknowledge several different categories of ancestors in Isese. These categories can be roughly divided into four main groups: Ase Afin (direct ancestors), Iyalode Alase (ancestral mothers), Ajala (civil chiefs), and Orisha (spirit protectors). Each category has distinct characteristics and importance in individual and communal religious practice. By recognizing each ancestor's role within Isese, individuals can form positive relationships and take on responsibilities between their past and present spiritual traditions.

### A. Ase Afin

Ase Afin, or direct ancestors, are those who have recently passed away, typically within the last four to five generations. These ancestors are seen as guardians of the family line and are venerated for their wisdom and strength. This is the most commonly recognized type of ancestor, and individuals are expected to pay their respects regularly through offerings and rituals.

### B. Iyalode Alase

Iyalode Alase, or ancestral mothers, are female ancestors venerated for their strength and courage. They are typically seen as the spiritual protectors of their descendants and their communities. Individuals are believed to receive guidance, protection, and blessings by honoring these female ancestors. As such, the veneration of ancestral mothers is essential for maintaining balance in the world.

### C. Ajala

Ajala, or civil chiefs, are the ancestors who were leaders in the community during their lifetime. These ancestors are remembered for their leadership qualities and courage, as well as their commitment to justice and protecting the people of their community. Venerating these ancestors is seen as a way to ensure the prosperity and continuity of the community.

### D. Orisha

Orishas, or spirit protectors, are supernatural entities with direct ties to the divine. It is said that these spirit protectors can act as intermediaries between the living and the divine and bring blessings to those who pay them homage. They are considered protectors of their descendants and the spiritual guardians of their family line.

Ultimately, honoring ancestors is an integral part of Isese. Through veneration and respect, individuals can ensure the spiritual protection of their family line and maintain balance in the world. This is done by offering prayers, making regular sacrifices, performing rituals, and showing respect to the ancestors. It's a way of showing reverence and gratitude for their wisdom and guidance, even in the face of adversity or hardship. By recognizing these ancestors and their distinct roles, individuals can find a deeper connection to the spiritual traditions of Isese and ensure the continuity of their family line.

## Identifying Your Ancestor

Identifying and honoring one's ancestors is an essential part of Isese, as it allows individuals to form meaningful relationships with their past. To do this, individuals must first recognize which category of ancestor they are venerating. This can be done through various rituals and ceremonies, such as ancestor worship and libation. Once the individual has identified the type of ancestor they are venerating, they can pay their respects and form a connection with them.

Through ritualistic offerings and prayers, individuals can honor their ancestors and maintain a connection to the spiritual aspects of their Isese heritage. This section will provide tips and advice on how to honor and connect with one's ancestors. It will also discuss the various rituals and ceremonies that can help individuals form a meaningful bond with their ancestors.

## A. Tips and Tricks

When honoring and connecting with one's ancestors, remember that the relationship should be a mutual exchange of respect. Individuals should pay homage to their ancestors through meaningful offerings and prayers while also listening for any messages or advice they might have.

In addition, remember that each ancestor should be respected in their own right. Different ancestors might require different offerings, prayers, and rituals to express one's gratitude. Here are some tips to keep in mind when honoring and connecting with one's ancestors:

- Offer up prayers to your ancestors. Prayers can be used as a form of honoring and expressing gratitude.
- Make offerings to the ancestors. This can be done through ritualistic activities such as libation, sacrifice, or ritual dance.
- Listen for any signs or messages from the ancestors. Many believe that the ancestors will send guidance and advice when needed.
- Show respect to the ancestors in your own way. Each ancestor is unique and deserves to be honored specially.
- Be open to the guidance and wisdom of your ancestors. They are a source of spiritual power and can provide great insight into life's challenges and struggles.

## B. Rituals and Ceremonies

Isese has a variety of rituals and ceremonies for honoring ancestors. Practitioners believe that the souls of their ancestors continue to influence their daily lives. They offer food, clothing, and other things to their departed ancestors, who are seen as mediators between human beings and the divine. During festivals such as Egunitogun, practitioners bring offerings of flutes and drums to pay tribute to the dead and give thanks tenfold for what they have been provided. Daily events take place at shrines dedicated to particular ancestors, where family members will offer prayers and sacrifices for continued guidance. The services help create a powerful connection between past generations and those living today, one which is highly valued and respected within Isese tradition. Here are some of the rituals and ceremonies used to honor one's ancestors:

- **Libation:** A ritual in which oil, water, or alcohol is poured onto the ground or a sacred object as an offering to the ancestors.
- **Sacrifice:** A ritual in which something is offered up for spiritual purposes, such as animal or food offerings.
- **Egunitogun:** A yearly festival wherein the living pays homage to the dead by offering flutes and drums in celebration.
- **Shrine Visits:** Visiting a shrine dedicated to an ancestor is a way of honoring their memory and expressing gratitude.
- **Prayer:** Prayers can be used to give thanks and ask for guidance from the ancestors.
- **Dance:** Ritualistic dancing and drumming are powerful ways of connecting with the ancestors.

### C. Connecting with Your Ancestor

Connecting with one's ancestors provides individuals with a deep connection to the spiritual traditions of their culture. It allows them to form meaningful relationships with their past and gain insight into their heritage. Through ritualistic offerings and prayers, individuals can honor their ancestors and maintain a strong connection to their spiritual roots.

The practices of honoring and connecting with one's ancestors are deeply ingrained in Isese culture. Here are some tips to help individuals connect with their ancestors:

- Keep an open mind and heart. Be open to whatever messages or advice the ancestors may offer.
- Meditate and practice mindfulness. This can help one become more aware of the subtle energies the ancestors may be trying to share.
- Create a sacred space for honoring the ancestors. This can be done by offering up prayers, offerings, and rituals to express gratitude and respect.
- Research one's ancestry and family history. Knowing more about the past can help bring the present into perspective and deepen one's understanding of their identity.
- Speak to a knowledgeable elder or spiritual leader about the customs and traditions practiced within Isese culture. This can provide deeper insight into the spiritual significance of

connecting with the ancestors.

Honoring and connecting with one's ancestors is an important part of Isese culture. Through meaningful offerings and prayers, individuals can pay tribute to their ancestors and maintain a strong connection to their spiritual roots. Regularly engaging in rituals and ceremonies can help create a powerful bond between the living and past generations that can provide strength and guidance in times of need. In honoring our ancestors, we honor ourselves and the legacy they have left behind.

By following the tips and advice discussed in this chapter, individuals can form a meaningful bond with their ancestors and gain insight into the spiritual aspects of Isese culture.

# Chapter 7: Honoring Your Ancestors

For generations, Isese people have held strong to the belief that their ancestors are still with them, watching and guiding them from beyond. This deep reverence for those who have come before carries through in many aspects of daily life in Isese villages, from offering prayers during meal times to celebrating events such as birth or marriage. As our ancestors carry us forward into tomorrow, we must never forget the ramifications and importance of honoring those who walked this path before us—something that the Isese people know only too well!

This reverence is an essential part of the spiritual, social, and cultural life of Isese. This chapter will provide a comprehensive guide on how to honor your ancestors in the Isese way. From offering Ebbo (sacrifices) to creating an ancestral shrine, we will cover all the main aspects of Isese ancestral veneration. You will learn what Ebbo is, the symbolism of Egungun (the Isese holiday for honoring ancestors), how to celebrate it, and the practice of ancestral meditation.

## Ebbo

Ebbo holds a vital place in Isese culture. It is a series of rituals that honor the gods and spirits and mark special occasions in the community. Traditionally, it can involve everything from singing and dancing to offering food sacrifices. All these rituals are done with intention and deep reverence for the deities they seek to honor. To those unfamiliar with their traditions, Ebbo might seem strange or even outlandish; however, it has a long history of keeping communities connected and secure in their identity. This powerful practice continues to be an essential part of Isese culture today.

## A. History of Ebbo

The Isese people, an ethnic group from West Africa, have a long and fascinating history with the Ebbo. This traditional religion dates back centuries and is still practiced today in Nigeria and other parts of West Africa. It centers around nature worship, ancestor veneration, rituals for sacrificing animals, moral values, and oracular consultations. Ebbo has changed over the years to accommodate modern technology, societal changes, and popular culture. Its symbols are worked into sculptures, paintings, jewelry, and theatrical performances. Even though it is not commonly known outside its origin countries, many Isese practitioners take great pride in their heritage and keep the faith alive by passing down stories from generation to generation.

## B. How to Perform an Ancestral Offering/Sacrifice

Isese culture is the traditional way of life used by certain Yoruba-speaking cultures. It focuses on reverence for the ancestors and their continued influence over society. A ritual for honoring and connecting with our ancestors is known as an ancestral offering/sacrifice. An Isese practitioner must understand the right way to perform this ritual to invoke ancestral blessings. Preparation will involve assembling items, including a calabash, several kola nuts, efun (white chalk) powder, and an onion. Once everything is ready, the individual begins chanting prayers and salutations to their ancestors before breaking the kola nuts into pieces and scattering them around the shrine area or place of sacrifice. After completing some libations (pouring of wine or water), the ancestral offering/sacrifice is complete!

## C. Symbolic Importance of Ebbo

Ebbo has many meanings and serves as a reminder of the people's heritage, faith, and beliefs. Ebbo is often used as a sign of spiritual protection, while other uses are more closely associated with promoting fertility. Ebbo can be used to honor ancestors and invoke their blessings and is seen as a source of strength, hope, and joy in everyday life, making it an integral part of Isese custom and tradition. The ritual of Ebbo is an essential part of Isese culture and a way to honor their ancestors.

# Egungun

Celebrating the Egungun Festival is a great way to come together and pay homage to Yoruba ancestors in Nigeria. It is an incredible tradition passed down through the generations and still holds tremendous importance today. One of the unique aspects of this cultural practice is when dancers dressed as Eguns join in the celebration, helping people remember their rich history. Festivities include vibrant colors, deliciously prepared traditional cuisine, rhythmic music, and plenty of dancing. It's a joyous occasion that allows us to reflect on our heritage while connecting with friends and family in our local community. So, if you have the chance, be sure to experience the Egungun Festival for yourself. It's one of those rare moments that will leave lasting memories and unforgettable stories for years to come!

### A. History of Egungun

Egungun is an age-old tradition of honoring ancestors in African Isese culture, believed to date back to the fifteenth century. Egungun festivals are typically filled with joyous and colorful dances, exquisite costumes, and commemorative speeches that honor and tell the stories of those who have passed before us. This tradition is rooted deeply in Isese society, provides a beautiful tribute to the deceased, and educates people about their culture and history. Each festival is unique, as each Egungun celebrates individual ancestry, allowing families and communities to come together to celebrate life from past to present.

### B. Customs and Symbolism Associated with the Holiday

Egungun is an integral part of Isese culture, and many colorful customs and symbols are associated with it. Different colors have meanings and add to the festive atmosphere when Egungun festivals are celebrated. Red is associated with royalty and power, while white symbolizes purity and peace. A popular dance style associated with Egungun is the ogogo, where the dancer wears the Egungun mask, and energetic music plays as they whirl around, stomping their feet in a detailed series of steps often known as "throwback" moves. The Egungun carries objects such as coconuts, beads, and kola nuts to demonstrate wealth and abundance to onlookers. It is sure to be an exciting experience for anyone who attends!

### C. Ideas for How to Celebrate Egungun

Isese culture celebrates Egungun through various festive activities. To properly celebrate the spirit, it is vital to honor those who have passed and show appreciation for their presence. One way to do this would be to carry out a special ceremony, full of drumming, song, and dance, in which members of the community follow steps traditional to Isese culture, such as wearing masks and colorful costumes. These costumes often feature intricate beadwork designs inspired by Yoruba art, adding beauty and bringing more joy into the atmosphere. Food is another integral part of every gathering, so a feast featuring different Nigerian dishes should be prepared so it can be shared with everyone. Finally, prayers can be offered throughout the day to honor their ancestors and thank them for their blessings. By participating in these meaningful ceremonies, people will better understand the importance of Egungun while still having fun and making lasting memories.

## Creating an Ancestral Shrine

Isese culture celebrates ancestral shrines as a place of gathering and reverence. Family members come together to give offerings and reflect on the lessons their ancestors have taught them. They view the shrine as where, even in death, the deceased is still part of the community, watching over their loved ones and offering guidance and protection from beyond. It is a peaceful, reflective time for individuals to celebrate their deceased relatives and embrace their rich culture. By honoring this tradition, family members honor their ancestor's memory and create an atmosphere of goodwill among themselves that keeps generations unified in love.

This can be created by placing items such as pictures, jewelry, and other mementos of their loved ones on a table or altar in the home. Some families may even create a permanent shrine in their yard or garden.

### A. Necessary Items for an Ancestral Shrine

When creating an ancestral shrine, a few items should be included. The first is a picture of the ancestor in question or a representation of them if one is unavailable. This will serve as the focal point for visitors and remind everyone of who their ancestor was. Other items that can be included are traditional Isese artifacts such as coins, jewelry, beads, ritual objects, and anything else that honors their memory. Finally, food offerings should be made to the deceased to thank them for watching over their descendants and offering love and guidance. By including these items, families can create a space of respect and love that will keep generations connected to their history.

### B. Placement of Items

The placement of the items is also crucial when creating an ancestral shrine. It is best to have the picture or representation of the ancestor in the central position, surrounded by other items of significance. The food offerings should be placed on the right side of the shrine to honor those who have gone before, and the objects should be placed on the left side to remember their legacy. Once these items are in place, keep the shrine clean and tidy as a sign of reverence. The shrine should be a place of serenity and strength, reminding everyone that even though their ancestors are gone, they remain in spirit.

### C. Rituals to Perform

Once the shrine is in place, it is time to perform rituals that honor their memory. Prayers and songs can be offered, along with incense burning to bring good energy into the home. Some families may perform traditional Isese dances or ceremonies to pay their respects. Lighting a candle can symbolize the deceased's presence in our lives and bring peace into the home. By participating in these rituals, family members will create a sense of unity and connection that will last for generations.

## Ancestral Meditation

Ancestral meditation is a tradition that dates back thousands of years and can be used to relax and reconnect with the ancient energies of our ancestors. It is believed that when we take the time to practice ancestral meditation, we are helping bridge a connection between our present selves and those who have come before us. Our ancestors passed on their knowledge, strengths, and experiences to shape who we are today and help make our lives worthwhile. Taking time to meditate regularly on this connection helps us appreciate their influence and provides powerful healing effects. It also gives us gratitude for all those who have gone before us and is part of the fabric of us as individuals. Give it a try—you will be glad you did!

## A. Purpose and Goal

Ancestral meditation practice is pursued to reconnect with one's family lineage and unlock the collective wisdom of ancestors. Developed by spiritual teachers, this form of guided meditation opens the door to deep spiritual awareness, healing, and transformation. Participants are brought back to their ancestral roots to explore their connection to an age-old lineage, bringing awareness to deeply held ancestral patterns, habits, and conditioning. As these anxieties and blocks are released, practitioners leave the experience feeling empowered and in harmony with the universe. With a wide range of techniques tailored to individual needs, ancestral meditation has become increasingly popular in exploring the personal and spiritual dimensions of existence.

## B. Preparing for the Meditation Session

When embarking on a journey of ancestral meditation, prepare and understand the steps for the practice. Start by creating a sacred space to honor your ancestors, and make sure you design it accordingly and with intention. Clear your mind, ground yourself, set intentions, and be mindful of timing when performing any rituals. Creating a ritual makes the process more intentional: It can help break away from an anxious state of mind while honoring spiritual memories safely. Take the time to get to know each ancestor and show gratitude for their existence, reflecting on how they impacted your life and still influence you daily. Ancestral meditation is an extremely rewarding journey. With patience, commitment, and understanding, you will surely find great joy in this practice!

## C. Steps for Ancestral Meditation Session

Bridging the gap between our current world and ancestors is easier than you might think with ancestral meditation. All it takes is a few simple steps to get started. First, you must find a quiet place and allow yourself to settle into a meditative state. Second, spend some time focusing on who your ancestors are or were and what values and views they may have held. Third, start developing a relationship by expressing gratitude for their presence in your life and moving on to ask for any guidance or wisdom they would be willing to share, anything from major life decisions to day-to-day challenges. And lastly, remember always to honor your ancestors as much as you can, keeping them close and in spirit all the time!

### D. How to End the Session

Ending a session of ancestral meditation can be a tricky endeavor; however, there are simple steps that anyone can take to make sure that the ceremony concludes in good spirits and an atmosphere of positive energy. The first is to thank the ancestors who have been present during the meditation. This act of recognition honors their sacred space and shows gratitude for their presence. The second step is to call forth and invoke any deities or angels invoked during the session so they may offer blessings five-fold for yourselves, your families, your friends, your ancestors, and all others in need. Lastly, allow everyone to recognize their unique relationships with the ancestors by briefly offering personal words of appreciation at the end of the session. Completing these steps before closing the session ensures that it will end in tranquility and mutual respect between the mediator, ancestor, and descendant.

### E. Benefits of Ancestral Meditation

Practicing ancestral meditation can bring about several important spiritual and personal benefits. These include improved self-awareness and emotional balance, increased understanding of one's spiritual lineage, and a closer connection with our ancestors. By aligning ourselves with the universal energies of our ancestors, we can access their wisdom and knowledge to help guide us in times of need. This meditation also gives us a greater appreciation for our family history, sense of identity, and the interconnectedness of all life.

Moreover, ancestral meditation can help us find meaning and purpose in our lives by uncovering our place in the grand scheme of things. Ultimately, this practice is a powerful way to bring us into harmony with our lives and those who have come before us. Through ancestral meditation, we can open ourselves up to a deeper understanding of our spiritual identity and gain greater insight into how we fit into the bigger picture. It is a practice that can profoundly affect our lives and relationships with those around us.

### F. Ways to Increase the Effectiveness of Ancestral Meditation

The effectiveness of ancestral meditation can be greatly enhanced by taking certain steps, such as:

- Focusing on the positive rather than the negative.
- Letting go of any expectations when starting the session.

- Setting an intention for the session, such as connecting with your ancestors or learning something new.
- Allowing yourself to be open and receptive to whatever information comes in during the session.
- Taking time at the end of the session to reflect on what you have learned and feel gratitude for your ancestors.
- Practicing regularly since consistency is key to deepening your connection with the ancestors.

The Isese practice of ancestral meditation is an ancient one passed down through generations. It is a powerful way to reconnect with our spiritual heritage and access the wisdom and knowledge of our ancestors. By engaging in this practice, we can develop a greater sense of self-awareness, emotional balance, and understanding of our place in the world. However, ancestral meditation should always be approached with respect and reverence for those who have come before us. By taking the necessary steps to create a positive and safe environment for our meditation sessions, we can ensure that this practice remains powerful and meaningful.

# Chapter 8: What Asafo Flags Can Teach

The Asafo flags of Ghana are a sight to behold! These vibrant pieces of art have been guiding communities along the coastal regions of the Fante people since the sixteenth century. Each flag is lovingly handmade, reflecting events that happened within each village and particular messages that need to be conveyed. Local chiefs can often be seen brandishing them during festivals and ceremonies as a sign of honor and respect. Through their intricate designs and bright colors, Asafo flags prominently stand as beacons of cultural identity within Ghana's historical landscape.

**Asafo flag.**

*Brooklyn Museum, CC BY 3.0 <https://creativecommons.org/licenses/by/3.0>, via Wikimedia Commons https://commons.wikimedia.org/wiki/File:Brooklyn_Museum_2009.39.1_Asafo_Company_Flag_Frankaa.jpg*

Asafo flags contain cultural meanings and narratives of the Fante people, located in the coastal regions of Ghana, and are commonly displayed at various social events, festivals (including Egungun), ceremonies, or even funerals. This chapter briefly explores the relevant cultural context of these flags. Then, we will discuss how people usually create them to transmit a message, parable, or moral. At the end of the chapter, you will find a few examples of flags with an interpretation of their meanings.

## Cultural Context of Asafo Flags

Asafo flags are vibrant and intricate works of art created by the Asante people of Ghana. These flags are more than just art. They represent the rich cultural heritage, social identities, and distinct personalities of each flag group. Asafo flags include pictures and symbols that tell a story about each group's beliefs, values, alliances, histories, honors, and rites. They also reflect an essential part of the oral tradition in West African culture as they convey messages through symbolism related to proverbs, historical events, and experiences that have shaped the Asante people. The mass production of these flags has made them a symbol of resistance against oppression and a vehicle for cultural reinstatement within contemporary struggles for justice and rights. If you ever see one, take in all it has to offer—a glimpse into a culture filled with beauty and resilience!

### A. Traditional Significance

Asafo Flags are traditionally used for various purposes, such as to mark the boundaries of a village, signal the location of an important meeting or event, or honor the dead. These flags serve as a reminder of traditional values and can be found at many festivals, funerals, weddings, and other special occasions. Asafo flags have also served as a form of protection from enemies, danger, or bad luck. The symbols on the flags are believed to have magical powers that can ward off evil spirits.

### B. Symbolism

Asafo Flags contain symbols and images that convey a message or moral lesson. These flags often depict animals and other natural elements, such as the Sun, Moon, and stars. Symbols of unity, such as hands clasped together, two brothers embracing, and a single bird perched on a branch, are also commonly seen. Other symbols convey messages of honor, respect, peace, unity, courage, and strength.

### C. Creation and Display

Asafo flags are usually created by the village chief or a group of elders and are handsewn with colorful cloth or fabric. They are then displayed at various events and hung in prominent places, such as on the walls of village homes or in front of public buildings. Asafo flags are usually proudly displayed at social events, such as funerals, weddings, and festivals. They often feature prominently in traditional processions or parades, signaling the start or end of a special event.

### D. Modern Significance

Asafo flags are now widely recognized and celebrated in Ghana and beyond. These flags are seen as symbols of pride, cultural identity, and resilience in the face of adversity. They have come to represent a shared history, heritage, and culture that can be passed down from generation to generation. Asafo flags are also used in a variety of creative art forms, such as photography, fashion, and design.

## Contemporary Relevance

Initially created by the Asante people of Ghana in the eighteenth century to display battle tactics during war times and unite multiple villages, their flags remain relevant today. Visitors to Ghana thoroughly enjoy seeing patterns, colors, and symbols that tell stories of family ancestry, history, and tradition on the Asafo flags. They also serve as a reminder of their many roots. These flying symbols have been used for political and cultural expression, inspiring communities and providing an important connection with the past. The narrative behind these flags is timeless. Various aspects of them are found in literature, poetry, film, music, and visual arts throughout the country. Asafo flags have truly stood the test of time!

### A. Popularity and Recognition

Asafo flags have seen a massive surge in popularity and recognition over the past few years. Originating in Ghana, Asafo flags are an African textile art form traditionally used by warriors to rally troops and celebrate victories. Today, they can be found all around the world as symbols of positive energy, bravery, and strength. Asafo flags stand as beautiful reminders of African culture and traditions, beloved for their bright colors and creative designs. They make for great conversation pieces for homes and workspaces. Whether it is simply a way to spread positivity or to honor one's heritage, Asafo flags offer something special that captures imaginations everywhere.

## B. Education and Cultural Preservation

Asafo flags are colorful traditional artifacts of the Akan people of Ghana. Although originally used in wars, today their significance has grown far beyond battle and spilled into contemporary life, playing a role in education and the preservation of cultural heritage. Asafo flags capture stories, symbols, and motifs that serve as both a documented history for subsequent generations and a visual reminder of past events. By displaying these artifacts to children, families can help to foster an understanding and knowledge of ancestry through educational dialogue and storytelling. Not only will this ultimately promote cultural engagement among Akan youth, but it also constitutes a lasting connection to their roots durably preserved in artwork unrestrained by written language. Undoubtedly, Asafo flags remain an integral part of cultural self-expression and identity that is essential to preserving the heritage alive.

## C. Asafo Flag Art

Asafo flag art originated from the Akan people in Ghana and is still used today to represent the warrior spirit, community identity, and cultural nationalism of those from West Africa. The flags are created using brightly colored textiles, intricate patterns, and symbolic motifs with important meanings. Each symbol represents aspects of the group's social life, like bravery, courage, protection, values, and faith, all of which form an invaluable part of Akan culture. Asafo flag art may look stunningly simple on the surface; however, they carry hundreds of years of wisdom handed down through generations. Depending on whom you are talking to, these beautiful banners can tell many stories, whether it is a proud military display or a more ceremonial processional. They remind their observers of the power and beauty within West African communities and make for a delightfully positive reminder to cherish our cultures for years to come.

# Process of Making Asafo Flags

For centuries, vibrant and intricate Asafo flags have been crafted in the Ghanaian village of Nkusukum. These flags are handmade with local materials such as raffia, cotton fabric, beads, and shells. While each is unique to its maker's village, all Asafo flags feature depictions of various animals to represent the beliefs and experiences of a particular community or organization. The process begins with sketching the artwork on graph paper and then transferring it onto the fabric using a tracing wheel before finally hand-stitching every detail onto visible pattern pieces. Once complete, the flag is ready to be used in special ceremonies made famous by Ghanaians everywhere.

### A. Materials

Creating an Asafo flag is a unique and special process. From start to finish, each flag component carries its symbolism, importance, and history. To bring the project together, however, many materials are required. This includes fabric, brightly colored samples of Kente cloths, or plain pre-dyed cotton. Additionally, beads must be found or purchased to represent certain symbols or techniques used on the flags. Most importantly, the Ashanti knotting technique is necessary to tie all of these components together into something special. You can ensure your completed Asafo Flag captures its intended meaning with great care and attention to detail!

### B. Design and Motifs

Design plays a major role in the process of making Asafo flags. From bold geometric shapes to intricate details, each flag is crafted with exceptional care. Colors often have symbolic meanings and illustrations representing a tribe's values or historical events. Inspiration for the designs comes from traditional African symbols such as Adinkra and Akan stamps, vibrant fabric cloths, and abstract representations of everyday life. The bold motifs are meant to be powerful declarations of pride for each tribe and honor their traditions. Crafting Asafo flags is an incredible art form that celebrates culture, creativity, and history.

### C. Color Palettes

Asafo flags are important to Ghanaian culture and form part of the country's vibrant visual art scene. One of the key elements in their intricate beauty is the unique use of color palettes. The artists that create these stunning works of art stretch their imaginations to assemble striking combinations, which can incorporate several different shades to bring out a range of emotions. Given the traditional spiritual meaning behind each color, it makes sense why such time and effort are put into creating each flag. Therefore, when we view an Asafo flag, we do not just see something beautiful; we see a meaningful piece of art crafted with skillful precision and contemplation to honor its associated gods or community history.

# Messages Transmitted through Asafo Flags

Asafo flags are brightly colored banners with distinctive patterns used to communicate messages in the Fante tradition of Ghana. Many of these symbols represent abstract concepts such as courage, strength, leadership, and unity, while others will announce a wedding or even advertise a local business. Every flag has a unique design and color combinations that were thoughtfully created to express each message, no matter the content. Asafo flags add vibrancy and culture to communities in West Africa, creating beautiful landmarks that remind us of the importance of heritage no matter where we originate.

### A. Narrative Art

Asafo Flags have been around for centuries and convey messages through an artistic medium. Narrative art has captivated people of many different cultures throughout history. Asafo Flags, which originated in Ghana and Togo among the Akan people, are no exception. Through their vibrant colors and intricate designs, these flags tell vivid stories that encapsulate important values within their villages or regions. They may include symbols from their past, such as battles won or deities worshiped, reminding the viewer of how far their culture has come. The display of these flags is quite a spectacle. It is truly inspiring to witness the dynamic beauty of Asafo flags passing by in a parade!

### B. Parables and Morals

Off the coast of Ghana, Asafo flags, also known as soldier's flags, are a feature of the culture in the Ga-Adangme region. They are beloved within their communities and crafted with beautiful fabrics. However, they're far more than objects of admiration. Each flag is said to carry with it a secret meaning. A moral is transmitted through symbols, patterns, and images on the flag. Much like a parable, this imagery conveys something greater than what can be seen. Each serves as an immortalized aid for local villagers to consider various life scenarios and ponder their inherent pros and cons. In this way, Asafo flags have been used for ages to commemorate bravery, express community values, and serve as additional subjects for conversation during social gatherings.

# Examples of Asafo Flags

Asafo flags are made with brightly colored fabrics and filled with symbolic motifs. Depending on the context, they come in various shapes, sizes, and designs. Some flags are rectangular, while others feature the traditional triangular shape. Some have a combination of both shapes. The popular symbols on most flags include animals, gods, and symbols of courage or strength. Additionally, some Asafo flags are made with a specific meaning in mind, such as celebrating war victories or honoring the death of a leader. Here are some examples of Asafo flags:

- The Adomabenu Flag features an elephant on the red side, representing strength and courage.
- The Sankofana Flag features a black-and-white striped pattern with the image of a leopard to represent leadership.
- The Akosua Adwoa Flag features a combination of yellow and purple triangles, symbolizing unity and collaboration.
- The Denkyem Flag features the image of a crocodile on the blue side, representing wisdom and adaptability.
- The Nsoroma Flag features a combination of white and red rectangles, representing resilience and faith.

Asafo flags are a beautiful form of visual art and storytelling, with many symbols carrying significant cultural meaning. They provide a unique way of expressing the values of a certain region or village, and their beauty is undeniable. Seeing an Asafo flag parade is truly an amazing experience, and it is a great way to learn more about Akan culture and its many important values. Be sure to check out some of these unique flags the next time you are in West Africa!

# Chapter 9: Iwa, or Building a Strong Character

Iwa Pele is an important concept in the Ifa tradition that focuses on a person's character or mental and moral qualities. Originating from the Yoruba people of Nigeria, Iwa Pele is a way to reinforce one's good character and work toward obtaining favor from the ancestors. It is a complex concept that has been passed down through generations and remains an integral part of the Ifa tradition today. This chapter will explain the origin and meaning of Iwa Pele, discuss its importance in the Ifa tradition, and outline the characteristics and benefits of a good character, as well as how one can attain this, according to Odu Ifa.

## Definition of Iwa Pele

Iwa Pele is a term native to the Yoruba people of Nigeria. It is the idea that by doing the right thing, showing integrity in one's actions, and striving to be the best version of ourselves, we can attain a sense of peace and oneness with our higher power. Iwa Pele can apply to all aspects of life, including faith practices, relationships, careers, and more. No matter what or whom we interact with, it's thought that having respect and adhering to good morals will enhance our purpose as humans in this life.

## Origin and Meaning

The phrase "Iwa Pele" has special significance in the Yoruba culture of Nigeria and translates to "good character" in the Yoruba language. The phrase reflects the collective elements that Yoruban people value as important traits: Honesty, humility, patience, respect, and strength. These values are ingrained in their everyday lives, aiming to foster strong relationships between individuals and create a harmonious environment within their community. Iwa Pele reminds people to strive for good character and behavior despite any difficult situations they might face. This notion helps instill resilience within each individual and recognizes the holistic importance of being well-rounded individuals contributing positively to society.

## Significance in Ifa Tradition

The traditional Ifa faith is based on the idea of Iwa Pele, a phrase that means "the character of perfect behavior." In the Ifa faith, Iwa Pele refers to respect, honesty, and accountability in all aspects of life. It serves as a code of ethics that guides believers to make the right decisions in their lives. Furthermore, if one follows the teachings of Iwa Pele, they may gain access to divine help and support from Orunmila (the God of wisdom). Ultimately, Iwa Pele is an integral component of the Ifa tradition and serves as a moral compass for those adherents hoping to find spiritual enlightenment.

## Characteristics of a Good Character According to Odu Ifa

According to Odu Ifa, a good character consists of several elements. These include respect for one's ancestors and humanity, the willingness to seek knowledge and wisdom, resilience in the face of adversity, and integrity through honesty and accountability. Additionally, a good character should have courage, patience, and dedication to doing what is right, no matter how difficult it may be. Lastly, Odu Ifa emphasizes being somebody with a kind heart that will never harm anyone, someone whose heart knows no boundaries or prejudices when it comes to loving others. With these qualities in our lives, we can certainly grow into true individuals respected among family, friends, and our community. Here are some ideas on how to develop and sustain a good character according to Odu Ifa:

### A. Respect

Adopting an attitude of respect for the beliefs and opinions of others is essential to developing a strong moral character. Respecting people's boundaries is key when fostering healthy relationships and building trust. This idea is even more relevant when interacting with people from different backgrounds and cultures. We need to recognize our differences and embrace them instead of trying to ignore or devalue them.

### B. Know Thyself

Self-awareness is essential if we are to grow into well-rounded individuals. Spend time reflecting and understanding your motivations, strengths, weaknesses, and values. Recognize the areas where you can grow and develop, and use this knowledge to better yourself. In the process, you will gain greater respect for yourself and those around you.

### C. Live with Integrity

A strong moral code is rooted in upholding integrity. To live with integrity is to always act according to your values and beliefs, regardless of the situation you may be facing. This means living with honesty and accountability for your actions. Essentially, it is striving to be the best version of yourself in all aspects of life.

### D. Persevere

Life can be full of obstacles, and many times it may seem easier to give up than push forward. However, having resilience and perseverance is key if we are to develop good character. Acknowledge the challenges that come your way as an opportunity for personal growth and development, and strive to take them on with strength and courage.

### E. Compassion

Compassion is a powerful tool that should not be overlooked when striving to become a person of good character, and being compassionate means having empathy and understanding for those around you and being willing to forgive those who have wronged you. This is a crucial part of the Ifa tradition that should be remembered. Remember, kindness and love are the foundations of a strong moral character. With these values firmly in mind, we can strive to be our best selves and reach our highest potential.

Ultimately, developing a good character is an ongoing process that requires effort and commitment. By following the teachings of Odu Ifa, you can create a strong moral foundation that will guide you throughout life. Respect, self-awareness, integrity, and perseverance are integral components of a good character that will lead to spiritual growth and enlightenment.

## Benefits of Having Good Character

Having a good character can result in truly amazing and positive outcomes. In terms of relationships, having a strong moral foundation and values can attract people who are similarly aligned and create more meaningful connections than those built on mutual convenience alone. This can lead to meaningful interactions with family, friends, coworkers, or significant others. On the professional front, having strong personal values, an honest work ethic, and reliable performance, can open up even more doors for success. People with good character will often be trusted by employers and given greater autonomy or responsibility within their position. Overall, having a good character is essential for creating meaningful connections in relationships and unlocking better opportunities for success in life.

### 1. Obtaining Favor from Ancestors

Having a good character is essential for attaining favor and blessings from our ancestors. Odu Ifa teaches that those who live with integrity and honor their ancestors will, in turn, be favored with spiritual protection and guidance from them. So, by living a life of good character, we can ensure that our ancestors are looking out for us and guiding us in the right direction.

### 2. Setting an Example

Having a good character means setting a good example for those around you. By living with strong values, treating others with respect, and having a moral code based on integrity, we can inspire those around us to do the same. This creates a ripple effect that can spread throughout society and lead to a better world for everyone. Our responsibility is to lead by example and create a legacy of good character that will last well beyond our lifetime.

### 3. Mental and Physical Well-Being

Having a good character is linked to better mental and physical health. Studies have shown that those with strong moral values experience less anxiety, stress, and depression. They also have higher self-esteem and overall better well-being than those who do not take the time to develop a strong character. Additionally, having a code of moral values can help keep us on the right path and make it easier to make decisions in our best interest.

### 4. Spiritual Fulfillment

Having good character is essential for finding spiritual fulfillment in life. By living a life of honesty, integrity, and respect for everything, we ensure that our actions align with the universe. This is essential for attaining spiritual enlightenment, as we need to ensure that our actions reflect the divine truth of the universe. We can strive toward a more connected and meaningful existence with these spiritual principles in mind.

### 5. Better Sense of Self

Most importantly, having good character can help us to understand ourselves better. By developing a strong moral foundation and following Odu Ifa's teachings, we can learn more about who we are, our true values, and beliefs. This can be very empowering, as it gives us the confidence to stay true to ourselves and follow our path in life. With a strong sense of self, we can make decisions that align with our values and morals, which can lead to even greater success in life.

## How to Attain Good Character

Achieving a good character involves developing strong morals and self-discipline. To maintain these solid foundations of moral strength, starting with small changes you can make daily is critical. This could be something as small as always keeping your word or taking responsibility for your mistakes. However, these habits become invaluable over time since they help us build important qualities like honesty, courage, and respect. Additionally, taking action when facing difficult decisions and situations toughens our character further by allowing us to reach beyond our comfort zone. In the end, attaining good character comes down to slowly adding values such as trustworthiness and determination into our behavior while also gaining different knowledge from every new experience we encounter.

### A. Education on Ifa Practices and Principles

One of the best ways to build a strong character is to educate oneself on Ifa practices and principles. Odu Ifa guides how to live an honorable and balanced life, which is essential for crafting good character. It also helps to develop respect toward the universe and all living beings, which is an incredibly important part of character building. Various resources are available to help us understand the teachings of Ifa and apply them to our daily lives.

### B. Self-Mastery

Another important way to build good character is through self-mastery. This involves taking the time to assess our behavior and attitude and finding ways to improve them. Self-mastery is about understanding our strengths and weaknesses to make a conscious effort to improve ourselves. This process ultimately leads us to a better character, allowing us to take control of our actions and ensure they align with our values.

### C. Prayers to Ancestors

One of the main ways to attain a good character is through prayers and offerings to our ancestors. Praying to our ancestors strengthens our spiritual connection and opens us to their wisdom and guidance. This helps us to stay on the path of virtue, which is essential for good character. Additionally, praying to our ancestors makes us feel more connected and grateful for their guidance.

### D. Engaging in Traditional Rituals

Engaging in traditional rituals is another powerful way to build a good character. Traditional rituals are often steeped in culture and spiritual significance, making them incredibly powerful tools for self-reflection and personal growth. By engaging in traditional rituals, we can gain new insights into our behavior and attitudes, helping us to stay on the right path. These rituals can also help us better understand our underlying values and beliefs, which are key for attaining a good character.

### E. Meditation and Reflection

Finally, meditation and reflection are important tools for attaining good character. Meditation helps to clear our minds and allows us to gain greater insight into our behavior and decisions. This is invaluable for character building since it gives us the clarity that we need to make wise choices in life. Additionally, through reflection, we can gain a deeper understanding of our values and what is truly important to us.

By applying these practices, we build our character gradually until it becomes solid and virtuous. Remember that character building takes time and effort; however, the rewards are worth it in the end. With a strong character, we can face any situation in life with confidence and grace.

Character building is an essential part of life that involves cultivating values such as trustworthiness, determination, respect, and self-mastery into our behavior. Educating ourselves on Ifa practices and principles, engaging in traditional rituals, praying to our ancestors, practicing self-mastery, and meditating and reflecting are all key ways to become the people we wish to be. By consistently following these practices, we can work toward attaining a good character that will serve us throughout our life.

# Chapter 10: Practicing Isese Every Day

Isese is an ancient African spiritual tradition practiced for thousands of years. It embraces the interconnectedness of all life and teaches that the spiritual, physical, and mental realms should be in harmony to bring about true joy and contentment. Practicing Isese involves incorporating its wisdom and worldview into one's everyday life. In this chapter, we will discuss various daily, weekly, and yearly rituals as well as other practices that can help deepen one's spiritual connection and improve their life through Isese.

## Daily Rituals

One of the most important aspects of Isese is that it encourages practitioners to be mindful in all they do. This includes taking time each day to gather one's thoughts and focus on the spiritual world. This can be done through prayer, mantras, chants, or other practices that help to quiet the mind and bring one closer to their spiritual self. Here are a few examples of daily rituals one may practice:

- **Meditation and reflection:** Take time each day to sit in stillness and reflect on the day's events. Think about how your actions have affected those around you and ask for guidance on how to serve better in the future.

- **Prayer:** Speak to your higher power and ask for guidance in all aspects of life. You can also ask for blessings for yourself and those around you. If you need help with a particular problem, ask for assistance.
- **Chanting:** Chanting is a powerful tool to create positive vibrations that can help fill your entire being with peace and joy. You can chant your prayers or those of your ancestors.
- **Journaling:** Writing down your thoughts and experiences can help clarify what is on your mind. It is also a great way to express gratitude for all you have been blessed with. Write down your positive affirmations or any other words of encouragement that can help you stay on track.
- **Offerings:** Offerings are a way of giving back to the universe. By gifting small items, you show that you appreciate all that has been given to you. This can include food, flowers, incense, or any other items representing your gratitude.

## Weekly Rituals

Most practitioners of Isese have weekly rituals they follow. These are usually centered around a particular theme or intention and involve activities such as singing, dancing, and chanting. Here are a few examples of weekly rituals one may choose to practice:

- **Singing and dancing:** Isese encourages the use of singing and dancing as a way to express joy and spirituality. Take some time each week to sing and dance in celebration of life.
- **Music circles:** Gather with friends and family to play instruments, chant, and share stories. This is a great way to strengthen bonds and connect with others.
- **Fire ceremonies:** Fire ceremonies are a powerful way to renew and cleanse the spirit. They can also be used to honor deceased ancestors and make offerings.
- **Baths:** Taking baths with herbs and oils is a way to relax the body and soul. It can also be used for spiritual cleansing and ritual purification.
- **Shrine tending:** Taking care of shrines or sacred places is a way to show respect for your ancestors and spiritual forces. This can

involve cleaning, offering food, lighting candles, and more.
- **Celebrations:** Gather with friends and family to celebrate your ancestors, deities, and the cycles of life. This can involve feasting, storytelling, and exchanging gifts.

## Yearly Rituals

Yearly rituals are a great way to honor the cycles of life and connect with one's roots. These can include festivals, pilgrimages, and other events that celebrate the spirit of Isese. Here are a few examples of yearly rituals one may practice:

- **New Year Celebrations:** Gather with friends and family to celebrate the new year. This can involve feasting, storytelling, dancing, and more.
- **Odun Ifa:** This is one of the most important yearly festivals in Isese practice. It celebrates a new cycle of life and renewal. The event includes singing, dancing, and offerings.
- **Ugbodu:** This is a yearly ceremony that celebrates the ancestors. Offerings are made, and stories are told about the ancestors' deeds.
- **Iwure:** This is a yearly ritual of purification and cleansing. It is a way of thanking the gods and spirits for all that has been given.
- **Pilgrimages:** Take a pilgrimage to a sacred site to recharge your spirit and deepen your connection with the divine. This can be to a local sacred site or a long journey.
- **Ancestor Rituals:** Take some time each year to honor your ancestors and connect with the spirit of those who have gone before you. This can include offerings, rituals, and storytelling.
- **Harvest Celebrations:** Give thanks for the cycle of life and all that has been given. This can be done at home or in communal gatherings.
- **Solstice Celebrations:** Celebrate the changing of the seasons and the cycles of life. This can involve rituals, offerings, and time spent outdoors.

Regardless of the type of rituals one chooses to practice, the goal is always to create deeper connections with oneself and the divine. By engaging in these activities, one can find a sense of peace and fulfillment in life. Living an Isese life also involves making conscious choices that honor the spirit within. By living mindfully and with intention, one can find harmony and balance in all aspects of life. Remember that rituals are meant to bring joy and healing. Feel free to explore different types of rituals and find what works for you. With practice, your Isese rituals can become a place of peace, renewal, and connection.

## Other Practices

Isese is a way of life that involves other practices such as eating right, exercising, and spending time in nature. Eating right can involve eating foods that are natural, organic, and locally sourced. Exercise can help keep the body in balance and lessen stress. Spending time in nature is a way to connect with the divine and find peace. Other practices may include prayer, meditation, chanting, and divination. Here are some ways to connect with the spirit and find balance in life.

### Clothing

Wearing clothing that reflects your spiritual beliefs can help you stay in touch with the divine. This includes clothes made of natural fabrics and colors that connect you with the natural world. Symbols, such as ancestral marks and spiritual insignia, can be worn to honor your ancestors and spiritual forces. In Isese, it is also crucial to dress in a way that reflects humility and respect for the divine.

### Intentional Living

Living with intention means making conscious choices that honor the spirit within. This can involve avoiding habits or activities that go against your spiritual beliefs and choosing to live in a way that aligns with your values. It can also involve participating in activities that bring you joy and helping others whenever possible.

### Spiritual Practices

Engaging in various spiritual practices can help you stay connected to the divine. This can include praying, meditating, chanting, or engaging in divination. All these practices can help bring clarity and insight into your life and strengthen your connection with the divine. The Isese tradition also includes rituals celebrating life cycles, such as harvest festivals and solstice celebrations.

### Foods/Dietary Guidelines

Eating natural, organic, and locally sourced foods can help keep your body in balance and bring you closer to the divine. Foods traditionally eaten in Isese culture include fruits, grains, legumes, nuts, and vegetables. Dairy products, eggs, fish, and poultry are also consumed in moderation. Eating eggs and poultry should be done respecting the animals, and the meat should be obtained ethically. Additionally, avoiding processed and unhealthy foods can help keep the body in balance.

## Symbols and Objects of Power

Symbols and objects of power can be used to invoke the divine. These include talismans, amulets, crystals, sacred vessels, and other items. In Isese culture, these objects are used to honor the ancestors and invoke spiritual protection. They can also be used in rituals and ceremonies to honor the divine and recognize the power of the spirit. Additionally, these items can help bring clarity, insight, and guidance into one's life.

### Connecting with Nature

Spending time in nature is a great way to connect with the divine and find peace. Walking in the woods, swimming in a lake, or sitting in your garden can help you find balance and appreciation for the world around you. Additionally, connecting with plants and animals can help you gain insight into the cycles of life. This can bring clarity and understanding to your spiritual journey.

### Altars/Sacred Spaces

Creating an altar or sacred space in your home can help you stay connected with the divine. This could be where you pray, meditate, or perform rituals. Here, you can place symbols of your faith, photos of ancestors and spiritual guides, crystals, candles, and other items with special meaning. This sacred space can remind you of your spiritual journey and help to keep you in touch with the divine.

### Drumming and Dancing

Drumming and dancing are important spiritual practices in Isese culture. They can invoke the divine, honor the ancestors, and celebrate life's cycles. They can also invoke healing energy and manifest positive change in the world around you. By engaging in these activities, you can connect with the divine and find joy in life.

### Greeting the Dawn

Witnessing dawn is an important spiritual practice in Isese culture. It is believed that by greeting the dawn, you are acknowledging the power of the Sun and honoring your spirit. This practice can also be used to start each day with intention and gratitude, as well as give thanks for the blessings of the new day.

### Journaling

Journaling is an excellent way to stay connected with the divine. Writing about your spiritual journey, reflecting on your experiences, and expressing gratitude for the blessings in your life can help you stay connected to the divine. Additionally, journaling can be a great way to gain insight and clarity on your spiritual path.

### Community Practices

Participating in community practices is an important part of Isese spirituality. Gathering with others to celebrate festivals and holidays, performing rituals and ceremonies, and honoring the divine can help strengthen your spiritual connection. Additionally, gathering in the community brings a sense of belonging and unity that is essential for spiritual growth.

### Listening

Finally, listening is an important spiritual practice in Isese culture. Learning to listen to your intuition, the wisdom of your ancestors, and the guidance of the divine can be an invaluable part of your spiritual journey. Listening to what is being said without judgment or expectation can help bring clarity and understanding into your life.

### Healing and Divination Practices

Healing and divination practices are important spiritual traditions in Isese culture. Practices such as prayer, meditation, reiki, palmistry, and tarot can help bring healing and insight into your life. By engaging in these practices, you can gain clarity and understanding of your spiritual path while obtaining balance and harmony.

### Connection with Ancestors

Connecting with ancestors is an essential part of Isese spirituality. Honoring ancestors through prayer, ritual, and storytelling can help bring their wisdom and guidance into your life. Additionally, connecting with ancestors can bring a deeper understanding of your spiritual path and create a powerful connection to the divine.

# Other Practices Recommended by the Isese Tradition

The Isese tradition recommends other spiritual practices like fasting and vision quests. Fasting can be used to purify the body and is often used to honor the ancestors. Vision quests can be used to gain insight and clarity into life's purpose, challenges, and spiritual direction. By engaging in these practices, you can gain a deeper understanding of your spiritual path and connect with the divine.

The Isese tradition is rich with spiritual practices that can be used to deepen your connection with the divine. By engaging in these practices, you can find joy and healing in life and gain insight into your spiritual path. Additionally, these practices help bring balance and harmony to your life and manifest positive change in the world around you. By engaging in these spiritual practices, you can connect to the divine and embark on a powerful life journey.

# Bonus: An Isese Glossary

Now that you have finished reading the book, you may be wondering about some of the more difficult Yoruba words and terminology used. Do not worry; you don't have to remember them all! Below is a comprehensive list of all the more difficult Yoruba words and terminology that appears throughout the book, as well as their phonetic spelling and the page in which they can be found being discussed more in-depth.

1. **Abiku (pronounced ah-bee-Koo):** In Yoruba culture, an Abiku is a child who dies young and continually returns to their family.
2. **Adura (pronounced ah-doo-rah):** In Yoruba culture, adura is the act of honoring the gods in ceremonies and rituals.
3. **Ase (pronounced ah-say):** Ase is an important concept in Yoruba religion, and it refers to the power of the gods that can be used for good or ill.
4. **Babalawo (pronounced bah-bah-lah-woh):** Babalawo is a Yoruba priest specializing in divination and healing.
5. **Chango (pronounced Shahn-go):** Chango is an orisha associated with family, strength, and justice.
6. **Egungun (pronounced eh-goong-goong):** Egungun is a masquerade festival where participants wear colorful costumes and masks to pay homage to their ancestors.
7. **Elegua (pronounced eh-lay-gwah):** Elegua is an orisha associated with communication and transitions.

8. **Esu (pronounced eh-soo):** Esu is an orisha associated with communication between the gods and humans, as well as luck and protection.
9. **Ibeji (pronounced ee-bay-jee):** In Yoruba culture, Ibeji are the twin spirit children of a family who have died young.
10. **Ifa (pronounced ee-fah):** Ifa is an oracle system used to communicate with the gods and is composed of a large corpus of Yoruba poetry.
11. **Itefa (pronounced ee-teh-fah):** In Yoruba culture, itefa is the act of an individual asking for divine guidance in making a decision.
12. **Iwa Pele (pronounced ee-wah-peh-lay):** In Yoruba culture, iwa pele is the concept of personal character and morality.
13. **Obatala (pronounced oh-bah-the-lah):** Obatala is an orisha associated with wisdom and purity.
14. **Oggun (pronounced oh-goohn):** Oggun is one of the most important gods in the Yoruba religion and is associated with war, ironworking, hunting, and farming.
15. **Oko (pronounced oh-koh):** In Yoruba culture, oko is the practice of using charms and incantations to bring good luck and fortune.
16. **Olodumare (pronounced oh-loh-doo-mah-ray):** Olodumare is the most powerful Yoruba god and is seen as the creator of all living things.
17. **Olokun (pronounced oh-loh-koon):** Olokun is an orisha associated with the sea, wealth, and fertility.
18. **Ori (pronounced oh-ree):** In Yoruba culture, Ori is the divine part of a person's soul that connects them to their fate.
19. **Orisha (pronounced oh-ree-sah):** In the Yoruba religion, the orishas are supernatural beings who possess powerful and mysterious forces.
20. **Orunmila (pronounced oh-roon-mee-lah):** Orunmila is an orisha associated with wisdom and divination.
21. **Ose (pronounced oh-say):** Ose is an orisha associated with healing and medicine.
22. **Oshun (pronounced oh-shoon):** Oshun is an orisha associated with love, beauty, and the river.

23. **Oya (pronounced oh-yah):** Oya is an orisha associated with wind, storms, and fertility.
24. **Sango (pronounced sahn-go):** Sango is an orisha associated with thunder and lightning.
25. **Yemaya (pronounced yay-mah-yah):** Yemaya is an orisha associated with the ocean and motherhood.

# Conclusion

Isese is a spiritual practice with roots in Yorubaland, Nigeria. It is a way of life deeply connected to the worshipers' ancestors and the orishas or deities. For those who follow Isese, honoring this practice brings balance, knowledge, and understanding among various aspects of life. From honoring ancestral traditions to listening to the wisdom of one's elders, this spiritual practice links all generations, present and past, together as one.

The path to inner harmony with yourself and the divine is difficult but worth traveling. Isese can guide us on this journey, giving us the tools to connect with who we are and build relationships between ourselves, the orishas, and Olodumare. We also learn how to open our hearts to honor our ancestors, recognizing the legacy that connects us all. Through Isese's teachings of self-love, understanding, and compassion, we can discover lasting peace within ourselves and find comfort in embracing our cultural heritage.

The practice of Ifa divination is widely used in Isese. This tradition has been passed down for generations through oral teachings and written scriptures known as Odu Ifa. This form of divination is said to be the most ancient, as it predates all other forms of religion or spiritual practices. Through this practice, one can learn how to interpret their destiny, get answers to pressing questions, and develop a better understanding of the universe. Learning how to practice Ifa divination can help practitioners gain clarity, knowledge, and insight.

In Isese, the Seven Great Orishas are revered. These deities are seen as mediators between humankind and Olodumare, the Supreme Creator of all things in the universe. Each of these orishas has unique characteristics, symbols, rituals, and gifts to offer us. By showing them respect, we can receive guidance and strength from their presence in our lives.

Finally, Isese encourages practitioners to keep their ancestors close by honoring the path paved before us. This is done through various ceremonies and offerings, such as libations or commemorative feasts, which can bring a sense of peace and connection to our ancestors. By understanding the importance of their legacy, we can keep their memory alive and be guided by their wisdom.

This easy-to-read guide is an introduction to the practice of Isese, taking you on a step-by-step journey through various aspects such as Odu Ifa, the Seven Great Orishas, and honoring your ancestors. Topics also included Asafo flags, Iwa (building a strong character), and how to practice Isese daily. For further exploration, we added an Isese glossary for additional understanding of the terminology used throughout this guide.

We hope that by delving into Isese, you will have a greater appreciation and understanding of your cultural heritage and a deeper connection to the divine. With this knowledge, you can now make strides toward your spiritual journey, finding balance and inner peace. May Olodumare bless you on your way!

# Here's another book by Mari Silva that you might like

# Your Free Gift
# (only available for a limited time)

Thanks for getting this book! If you want to learn more about various spirituality topics, then join Mari Silva's community and get a free guided meditation MP3 for awakening your third eye. This guided meditation mp3 is designed to open and strengthen ones third eye so you can experience a higher state of consciousness. Simply visit the link below the image to get started.

https://spiritualityspot.com/meditation

# Bibliography

Alston, D. D. "Ifa Reading of the Year 2022-2023." Last modified June 10, 2022. https://www.daydreamalston.com/blog/tag/isese

Atla LibGuides. "African Traditional Religions: Ifa." Last modified December 15, 2022. https://atla.libguides.com/OER_Ifa

Spiritual Doctor AFI. "Virgo Season and the Orishas." Last modified September 7, 2019. https://spiritualdoctorafi.com/blog/tag/isese

www.ingramcontent.com/pod-product-compliance
Lightning Source LLC
Chambersburg PA
CBHW072153200426
43209CB00052B/1164